Better Homes and Gardens

the porch book

A **Better Homes and Gardens** Book
An Imprint of
WILEY

Published by John Wiley & Sons, Inc., Hoboken, New Jersey
Published simultaneously in Canada

Limit of Liability/Disclaimer of Warranty: While the publisher and the author have used their best efforts in preparing this book, they make no representations or warranties with respect to the accuracy or completeness of the contents of this book and specifically disclaim any implied warranties of merchantability or fitness for a particular purpose. No warranty may be created or extended by sales representatives or written sales materials. The advice and strategies contained herein may not be suitable for your situation. You should consult with a professional where appropriate. Neither the publisher nor the author shall be liable for any loss of profit or any other commercial damages, including but not limited to special, incidental, consequential, or other damages.

For general information about our other products and services, please contact our Customer Care Department within the United States at (800) 762-2974, outside the United States at (317) 572-3993 or fax (317) 572-4002.

Wiley also publishes its books in a variety of electronic formats and by print-on-demand. Some content that appears in standard print versions of this book may not be available in other formats. For more information about Wiley products, visit us at www.wiley.com.

Note to the Readers:
Due to differing conditions, tools, and individual skills, John Wiley & Sons, Inc., assumes no responsibility for any damages, injuries suffered, or losses incurred as a result of following the information published in this book. Before beginning any project, review the instructions carefully, and if any doubts or questions remain, consult local experts or authorities. Because codes and regulations vary greatly, you always should check with authorities to ensure that your project complies with all applicable local codes and regulations. Always read and observe all of the safety precautions provided by manufacturers of any tools, equipment, or supplies, and follow all accepted safety procedures.

ISBN 978-0-470-94852-1

Printed in the United States of America

10 9 8 7 6 5 4 3 2

BETTER HOMES & GARDENS BOOKS

Editorial Director
Gregory H. Kayko

Art Director
Tim Alexander

Executive Editor
Larry Erickson

The Porch Book

Contributing Editor
David Toht, Greenleaf Publishing, Inc.

Contributing Designer
Mary Pat Crowley

Contributing Illustrators
Ian Worpole
Rebecca Anderson

Contributing Proofreader
Hope Breeman

Better Homes & Gardens
Editor in Chief
Gayle Goodson Butler

Home Core Content Director
Jill Waage

Deputy Content Director
Karman Hotchkiss

Art Director, Home Design
Gene Rauch

Administrative Assistants
Heather Knowles
Sue Miller

JOHN WILEY & SONS

Publisher
Cynthia Kitchel

Acquisitions Editor
Pam Mourouzis

Production Supervisor
Marcia Samuels

Production Editor
John Simko

welcome

THAT'S THE MESSAGE OF A PORCH: Welcome in from outside. Welcome, friends and visitors. Family? Welcome home.

And that's the message of this book: Welcome to the warmth, charm, grace, comfort, and style of American porches. Welcome to the process of considering, planning, and building a porch of your own. It will surely add beauty, comfort, and value to your home.

A porch is more than a transitional space linking indoors and out. It's a buffer, a place to linger and enjoy your environment— gentle breezes, dappled sunlight, singing birds, and busy family—from the leisurely comfort of a space tailored to you.

In this book, you'll see the power a porch has to transform a home, through dramatic before-and-after photos and interviews with homeowners. You'll learn about architectural styles, construction fundamentals, and how to plan and equip your porch. And you'll visit jobsites to see the step-by-step process of porch-building.

In the end, we hope you'll take time to look back through these pages someday soon in the comfort and satisfaction of your own new porch.

contents

before and after

The transforming power of a porch can give a weary house new life. In this chapter you'll find a collection of **BEFORE-AND-AFTER SAGAS** that demonstrate what a difference a well-designed porch can make. Each porch illustrates a transformation strategy—and perhaps an important insight that will help reform your own porch. Often these transformations **ECHO ARCHITECTURAL DETAILS** already in the house, but buried in earlier remodelings. Pulling them out and enhancing them as key elements in a new porch returns the house to its roots, making it even more distinctive. Some of these porches **ADD ELEMENTS** such as columns, railings, and arbors never before seen on the house. The result is an updated look that refreshes the house and boosts curb appeal. Finally, these porches add **OUTDOOR LIVING SPACE** to extend a welcome, providing a setting for hospitality and retreat.

before

Let form follow function

A small concrete stoop outside the front door fell short of homeowner Nancy Tamres' dream of a front porch. "I definitely wanted a porch filled with my things, where I could read and relax," she says. The porch addition to her 1940s Cape Cod in Oyster Bay, New York, more than fit the bill, transforming a blank exterior and adding plenty of outdoor living space. Architect Pat O'Neil made the transformation by extending the home's roof to add the 7×32-foot porch. Landscape designer Georgia Waltzer put the finishing touches on the design, creating a stone path to the porch and filling the lawn with a variety of plantings. Nancy couldn't be happier with the results: "We have our coffee on the porch every morning before setting off to work."

TAKE AWAY

3 tips to remember

1 Emphasize the entryway with contrasting color.

2 Highlight the entry with a gate.

3 Small porches can make a difference.

before

Be understated

Guests shouldn't have to search for the entryway. Without a porch to signal its existence, the tucked-away front door on this 1930s Colonial was all but hidden from view. The addition of a modest porch made all the difference. In remodeling their home, Virginia and Reynolds Young learned that substantial changes aren't needed to achieve a dramatic look. The traditional pilasters and overhead pediment of their new porch captured the look of country cottages they saw during travels in England. The crisp lines of the entryway contrast with the brick tinged with white paint remnants, the result of workers blasting away the layers of paint that had covered the facade, leaving a weathered appearance. To complete the country-cottage transition, groundcovers replaced the lawn and thick ivy in front of the home.

before

Do a light upgrade

The essential look of this century-old home remains unchanged—most often a good idea when dealing with old homes. However, several subtle improvements take it to a new level. Doubled support columns add something extra to the porch's style and structure. New railings and balusters add architectural interest and bring the porch up to code. Old brick and concrete steps were excised, replaced by wooden steps that blend in with the railing. Centering the entry stairs on the gable by moving them a few feet provides a destination for a new, curved front walk. Stone veneer replaces the hard-to-maintain lattice panels beneath the porch.

3 tips to remember

1 Make the entryway architecturally distinctive.

2 Use a highly pitched roof as a focal point.

3 Soften predominating geometry with an arch.

before

Add a focal point

"This was a hundred-year-old farmhouse up on a hill with terrific views," says architect Jeffrey King. "And no personality whatsoever." The arched portico porch he added gives the house a much-needed focal point. The high-pitched roof of the portico emphasizes the entryway previously hidden under a glowering gable. Add to that the welcoming space of a full front porch with its gracious columns and a simple railing treatment and you have a porch with a truly transformative personality.

before

Complement a dominant feature

A grand gable of this 1920s clapboard house overwhelmed an afterthought of a porch. Atlanta architectural designer Frank G. Neely replaced the porch with a portico whose dramatic roofline complements the original gable. Taking inspiration from the interior's Arts and Crafts style, he added character-building porch details that reflect the home's heritage, including square columns joined by an eyebrow arch, corbels, a custom dark-stained mahogany front door, and lead-glass sidelights.

before

Pull forward

Cape Cods are known for their spare, no-nonsense profile, but that doesn't have to mean a flat, featureless facade. Effectively grabbing key elements and pulling them forward added interest and detail to this home. For example, the detailed fascia treatment and deep eaves project outward to lend dimension to the porch. The porch roof is an extension of the existing roof line—a great trick for melding old with new. The centerpiece of a whole-house redo, this lovely portico porch transforms a dull entryway into an eye-catching feature. The arched ceiling of the portico helps soften the severity. Red brick steps add a timeless touch and a sound base for the elegant columns. The brick patio signals that the front of the house can be a great place to linger.

BY DESIGN
Design for a point of view
Stagecraft can make all the difference. This porch is all about well-crafted illusion. All the elements—overhang, stanchions, walls, windows, landscaping—were upgraded and now work in concert to create the right impression.

before

Find opportunities in limitations

Strict zoning regulations kept a South Pasadena, California, homeowner from increasing the square footage of her home, leaving her with few options to update it. Then she made a discovery. Because posts supported her front porch, the size of the porch counted toward the home's overall square footage. By removing a front porch with posts, the homeowner was able to transfer that square footage to an addition at the back of the house. The new porch is part illusion but as good as the real thing. A postless cantilevered roof hovers over a decklike area. Substantial river-rock stanchions trick the eye into believing there are posts. River-rock walls extend the illusion.

Add a portico

After exchanging wedding vows on Martha's Vineyard, Susan Andrews and Phil Tubbs returned to their Kansas City–area home with ideas to add character to their plain Colonial house. Chief among them was a portico porch, which proved as practical as it was stylish. "We were tired of our packages—and our guests—getting soaked at the front door," Susan says. "We built the portico for protection, for practical reasons, but it turned out to be the thing that changed the look of the entire front of the house."

before

Age gracefully

Even though this house was less than 10 years old, the owners felt it was time to take it beyond builder basic. Adding a wraparound porch created a delightfully vintage look and added valuable outdoor living space. Arched detailing atop each post softens the starkness of the original house—a subtle but welcome relief from an abundance of straight edges. The gable above the porch steps gets its inspiration from the second-story roofline. Blue shutters help wind back the clock and add a much-needed punch of color.

before

before

Add on

This modest-sized Washington State Cape Cod badly needed an entryway that didn't look like a back door. The challenge was in finding a suitable solution without overwhelming the modest facade. A columned portico porch would have been overkill. Instead, a modest 48-square-foot bump-out centers the front door and adds a visually uplifting gable roof. A beamed overhang shelters without dominating. Low rock walls flank wide steps, beefing up the front door's presence. Landscaping aids the transformation: In its prior state, the small home was almost overtaken by pom-pom shrubs that crowded the house and encroached on the front steps. Ripping them out left room for low-profile plantings that add color and interest without stealing the show.

before

Dig for hidden character

The rooflines and traditional detailing on this home might convince any architecture buff that it's a century old, but it was actually built in 1986. Two great porches—front and back—are at the heart of its recent transformation. The basic bones were there—the bay windows and the bumpout dormers—but there was a hole where the front porch wanted to be. Architectural designers Karen Kallweit Graham and Ross Graham added a new gable above the front porch and flattened the pitch above the bays. New wood posts and masonry pillars support the gable and further accentuate the front entrance.

Extend and refresh

The porch added to the back of this home demonstrates the utility of a half roof: shade when you want it, plenty of room to bask in the sun during the shoulder seasons. Shingled piers add variety to the railing and help tie it into the second story. The stairway descends in easy stages, neatly tying in the ground-level patio. Shingle siding with new color and windows complete the transformation.

before

before

Attach a gazebo

Ken and Kerry Wable wanted a porch that would give their circa 1910 house in Pennsylvania more Victorian character. Ken, a general contractor by trade, has built many gazebos, but theirs was the first he had attached to an existing house. The porch is 7 feet deep and 18 feet wide, the gazebo 9 feet in diameter. Ken received a 2-foot variance from the local setback regulations so he could build the porch he envisioned. He included a new gable to call attention to the entry.

before

Deconstruct

Sometimes it's not what you add but what you take away. Floor-to-ceiling screens made this Atlanta porch gloomy. The homeowners opted to clean things up by removing the screens and adding fascia to cover the exposed rafter ends. Because the left side of the porch is only 24 inches from the ground, local building codes didn't require a railing. As a finishing touch, the zippy paint job brought the house to life. The candy-bright hue of the floor and new vintage-style screen door complement the yellow vinyl siding.

Refocus a feature

You know the saying "When life gives you lemons. . . ." But what if those lemons are a severe infestation of mold? Is there really a lemonade solution? For this 1990s "contemporary manor," the answer was yes. A flaw in the stucco siding caused so much moisture damage that the entire exterior was ruined. The owners seized the opportunity to give their home more warmth and traditional style—with a new entry portico as a focal point. They removed an overbearing transom above the entry, making way for the gabled portico. Stickwork in the gable echoes an arched transom atop the front door and an arch above the second-story windows. It all adds up to a beautiful porch that is a great place to relax.

before

3 tips to remember

1 A boring house is a blank canvas ripe for creative improvement.

2 Vertical elements like gables, stairs, and columns have the most visual impact.

3 Sketches and models (see *pages 84–91*) let you play with design ideas.

Wrap around

Starting with a boxy home that was anything but welcoming, Colorado homeowner Kyle McCoy designed this dramatic front-porch facelift and learned construction techniques along the way. With help from her son Nathan, 19, her father, and a revolving crew of skilled friends, she completed the project over a year's worth of weekends. Her key to do-it-yourself success? "If you take anything in steps, and take it slow, it's not so daunting." She replaced a brooding overhang with a gently arched portico. A gazebo wraparound adds outdoor living space and pleasing variation to the roof line. The family often enjoys dinner under the cool breezes of a ceiling fan in the gazebo section. "The porch makes the house feel so much bigger," Kyle says.

before

before

Dare to demolish

In its former life, the entryway to this Minnesota home was hidden on the flank of the solarium, making the mid-century modern anything but welcoming. All that changed when a gracious new porch replaced the solarium, adding a cottage look in sync with the home's lakeside location. Designer Gary Knight incorporated custom-detailed posts, a beaded-board ceiling, and square railings. To accommodate the newly elevated porch, Knight installed a rock retaining wall to build up the yard at the base of the porch. Stained ironwood decking complements the cedar siding, while cedar-stained steps direct the eye—and visitors—to a new, welcoming entryway.

before

Pull it all together

A fiercely symmetrical porch is often an anchor when the front of a house is going several directions at once. While not for every house, a straight-on symmetrical element like this porch brings order to chaos, a place for the eye to rest when it otherwise doesn't know where to go. We often talk about the porch as a miniature house in this book. This porch, packed with elegant detailing and supported by four firm columns, is an architectural gem. It pulls things together, including the crosshatched windows flanking the door—windows that would otherwise look out of place. The high gable melds the first story to the second, giving vertical lift to an otherwise horizontal house.

Create a destination

This Colonial-style home in Portland, Oregon, was begging for a front porch, notes building designer Kathy Kremer. She designed an entrance that complements the home's early-20th-century roots and lives up to the formality of its terraced gardens. Most importantly, Kremer's design gave the blank exterior an eye-catching feature. While turning the nearly invisible doorway into an inviting destination, she designed a hip-roofed structure with an open-ended gable centered over the transom-topped door. Kremer placed support columns to frame views of the doorway and sidelights. Lower-level shutters and enhanced landscaping complete the reformation.

Be mindful of proportion

Consider the historical style and scale of other homes in your neighborhood before renovating. To preserve the quaint scale of this house, a second-story addition was added to the back of the house. Its presence is evident from the front only by a shed dormer.

before

Add a few good things

Just a handful of strong elements can make all the difference. Adding a crisp overhang above the front door, coupled with a deep metal awning above the front windows, was all that was needed to bring out the latent storybook charm of this Austin, Texas, home. Suddenly, existing assets like the arched front door, brick facade, and curving roof line pull together to make a great house.

Color changes helped. The door was stripped of its paint and stained dark brown, while the variegated brick facade was smoothed and subdued with pale gray paint. The brick sidewalk from the street to the front door was rarely used because visitors walked to the entry from the driveway on the side of the house. That oft-traveled red brick path was replaced with tumbled gray pavers, and the front steps were stained a deep brown to better suit the new exterior color scheme.

before

Frame the front door

A columned portico porch forms the focal point for the whole-house remodel of a ho-hum bungalow. Echoing the pitch of the gable roof, the portico is airy and open. Its arch breaks up the geometry and beautifully frames the front door. New fascia treatment applied to the house is scaled down to suit the porch. The new portico is an anchor for classic touches like the multi-pane windows, slate-style fiberglass-composite shingles, black shutters, and a new walkway made from concrete stamped to resemble cobblestones.

TAKE AWAY

3 tips to remember

1 Echo unique features, like the archlike gambrel roof of this house.

2 Scale up new features to match the size of the facade.

3 Consider a window upgrade as part of your porch transformation.

before

Create an echo

This tall, austere home in the Northeast—nicknamed the Gray Torpedo by homeowners Linda and Denis Forster—had one advantage: It was mere yards from the ocean. Otherwise, the exterior of the vertical house had little to commend it. That all changed with a whole-house transformation centering on a new entryway. Echoing the gambrel roof of the house, the barrel-vaulted portico looks like it always was there. Previously, visitors entered through an inauspicious sliding glass door under a roof that connected the house and garage. Now they enter through a handsome porch supported by columns and graced by an over-the-door fanlight.

Filling the void

Previously, the face of this 1970s contemporary was anything but welcoming. The homeowners enlisted designer Lori Zajic to improve the situation, asking her to keep costs down by staying within the original footprint. She responded by adding a stunning Craftsman-influenced porch. She made no other structural changes, even reusing the existing concrete steps. Cedar planks salvaged from a deck elsewhere on the property were sanded and refinished to become the beautiful porch floor.

before

Look backward

Beneath a shell of faded aluminum siding, the bungalow style of this Des Moines home was just waiting to come up for air. Inspired by a book of home designs from the 1920s, the homeowners decided to open up the enclosed porch while keeping the roof intact. Pyramidal columns add vintage-looking support for the ceiling, while new windows evoke the period of the home. A new deck area, a weighty set of steps, and a brick walkway also create a fresh approach to the entry.

before

Bank on the curves

No doubt about it: Any sort of arch is complicated to build and will add to the cost of your porch. However, its impact is dramatic, a transforming feature that can lift your home out of the ordinary. Before you rule out an arch, consider economizing on other features. The purchase of upscale light fixtures, house numbers, and door hardware can wait—they're easy to install later. Simple prefab columns can serve until your budget can manage custom-made replacements. A railing may not be necessary if your porch is less than 30 inches above grade. If it is required by code, consider a temporary railing made of 2×4s and 2×2s for the short term. In the meantime, your entryway arch will more than carry the day.

before

Accent with an arch

The homeowners loved the wooded seclusion of their Birmingham, Michigan, home but weren't enamored with its American Colonial look. Instead, they took it in a Craftsman direction, adding a beautifully arched portico with handsome fluted pillars that echo the existing pilasters. With the arched entryway as a focal point, it made sense to expand the porch area for new outdoor living space. Combined with a new bank of front windows, sunflower-yellow paint on the trim work, and a meandering front walk, the porch successfully takes the home from austere to awesome.

Let nature lead the way

Draw color and material-choice inspiration from nature—green trim, cedar shake–style siding, and river rock walls combine to help this new exterior fit into its woodland surroundings.

before

Stretch out

A treacherous tile drive and aging aluminum windows left the facade of this Orinda, California, home devoid of charm. Still, the new owners spied potential in the property's lush surroundings, envisioning a gracious porch stretching elegantly across the front of the house.

The design team extended the roof forward and stretched the original landing to create an expansive porch. New 6×6-inch porch posts are rhythmically spaced 6 feet apart. Two posts strategically flank the front door. Natural rock and pillars featuring exterior lanterns grace the tiered steps leading to the front door, replacing old red bricks.

Combine pergola and portico

A tree-filled lot is something to cherish, but it can put your home's interior in the shade. When the owners of this Des Moines home launched into a porch transformation, they wanted the spaciousness of a full front porch while still letting sunlight into their front windows. The answer: a pergola overhead structure combined with a portico entryway. The pergola mimics the look of a full-size front porch, while letting the light in. (As a bonus, it saved the cost of a sheathed and shingled roof.) The widened portico supported by pairs of columns is scaled up to suit the house.

before

Like a house in miniature

Any porch has all the elements of a house—foundation, walls, and roof. That means that without much additional investment you can sometimes stretch those existing elements of the house forward to create a new porch.

before

Extend outward

The small, lackluster entry on this 1912 Houston bungalow failed to extend a gracious welcome. Determined to put their home's best face forward, the owners did away with the original stoop and overhang, replacing them with an expansive 8×27-foot veranda.

Thanks to an extended roof line and the porch's spaciousness, the whole house now looks larger and more distinctive. Four stout Craftsman columns do their part to amplify the facade's visual heft while adding style points reminiscent of the home's heritage. Crisp white railings, a sweeping set of stairs, and a brick-paved entry courtyard provide the finishing touches to the makeover.

before

Add a veranda

A too-flat facade stunted the true potential of this Cape Cod home in Marblehead, Massachusetts, spurring its owners to think bigger and better. Eager to enhance the abrupt entry and provide more outdoor living space, they extended the roofline to create a sprawling L-shape veranda and expanded breezeway. Following the lines of the home's main-level windows, the new roofline melds seamlessly with the original architecture. Stout columns support the expanded roof while dentil molding adds a gracious vintage flavor perfectly in step with the rest of the neighborhood.

TAKE AWAY
3 tips to remember

1 Return your home to its architectural roots.

2 Remove prior remodelings that wandered off point.

3 Revive original elements worth keeping.

before

Return to roots

The charm of this turn-of-the-century Elk Mound, Wisconsin, house was kept under wraps for 40 years, following a not-so-sensitive exterior remodel in the 1960s. To revive the home's architectural heritage, the owners replaced a dark and dated enclosed porch with a sweeping (and more historically accurate) wraparound, installing breezy custom railings where walls once stood.

After doubling the footprint of the enclosed porch and laying gleaming fir floorboards, they added a new secondary entrance that allows easy access to living spaces inside. New shutters and low-maintenance vinyl siding complete the overhaul, making the home's entryway more vibrant and engaging.

Winner by a nose

Pleasing architecture plays on the best features of the human form. Without a nose, this house presents a blank expression to the world. A vacant appearance is often a clue to where new emphasis is needed.

before

Add dimension

"We looked past the typical shoebox construction and imagined the house with the facade it deserved," Jenny Kopach says of her Chicago-area Colonial. The flat-face home was longing for some extra dimension, and adding a covered porch gave the facade the depth it needed. Double columns anchor the porch, and its roomy proportions make it a fully usable outdoor room.

This porch follows several good architectural principles. Its roof is as high as the home's main-level ceiling, so the porch doesn't block views from the front rooms. The columns and railing are similar in style and scale to the home's original trim, and they're painted the same color. Finally, the porch's overall size suits the existing house. The roomy but understated full-length porch the Kopaches opted for grounds the home, giving it a gracious, welcoming presence.

Add texture

Although neglected and forlorn, this Atlanta Cape Cod had good bones—and a beautifully wooded lot. Homeowners Joe and Sylvia Gayle believed it could be transformed into a Craftsman-style cottage. To achieve this, architect Bill Harrison removed the utilitarian shed entryway and added a new front porch incorporating Tudor Revival and Craftsman features. The homeowners wanted the result to have a look of permanence—not appear to be a recent remodel. The river rock facade does the trick. To meld the porch to the house, the rock carries through to the foundation as well. Sweeping stairs and an ample landing benefit from a iron railing with a beautiful branch motif—a great choice for the wooded setting.

before

Renew with finishing touches

Sometimes it doesn't take a lot to transform a porch. Earlier remodeling efforts erased much of the character of this turn-of-the-20th-century home, including the choice to screen in a once-expansive front porch. By nixing the screens and adding a new railing treatment, the gracious openness of the porch was restored. The biggest change was facing the pillar bases with stone, adding warm color and rich texture. An updated paint treatment completes the new look.

before

Double up

Stairs projecting forward from the landing of this suburban Chicago screened porch would have stolen valuable backyard space. As an alternative, the owners added twin staircases on either side of the landing, not just a convenience but a great-looking design as well. A low-slung hip roof and deep eaves help meld it to the house, taking the edge off the contemporary detailing of the porch. In keeping with the earth tones of the brick, the porch is built of cedar, sealed to retain its beautiful golden color. Cedar heartwood naturally resists weather-related rotting as well as bug infestations.

before

before

Add a balcony

It may have been the wraparound porch or the master bedroom's glimpses of a nearby lake, but when this Michigan home came up for sale, Rick and Linda Wertz were enticed by its possibilities. They bought it with plans to renovate and sell. The front porch not only was dowdy, it had serious structural problems. The couple rehabbed the porch and added a balcony outside the master bedroom to capitalize on the view of the lake. Accessible now through French doors, the balcony serves as a small outdoor escape. A brick paver pathway, fresh paint scheme, and eye-catching planter boxes give the home an all-American appeal. The outcome was so remarkable, the Wertzes sold their other home and now call this one the keeper.

Seize the openings

Openings like the small gable window and porthole windows on the sides of the entryway add interest to blank areas. You'll appreciate the light inside as well as the engaging appearance of the porch as seen from the street.

before

Bring out the beauty

Somewhere beneath the neglected facade of the 1933 bungalow he purchased, Ric Parrish saw potential. Along with Matthew Quinn, Ric set out to renovate the house inside and out. Although the house was architecturally stable, improving the exterior was a major priority. Ric and Matthew added to and subtracted from the original to create a style they call "American eclectic bungalow." They extended the entryway, adding a portico supported by triple Tuscan-style columns and featuring built-in benches. A new front door is flanked by budget-sparing faux sidelight panels. Wide orchard-stone steps and handsome planters add an upscale touch.

before

Make the staircase a feature

When they saw the porch and staircase that wrapped awkwardly around an old tuck-under garage, Sylvia Lindstrom and Don More took pity on the house they were considering and decided to restore its original character—with a twist. Enlisting the help of designer Robert Patterson, the couple removed the after-thought staircase and landing, and replaced it with a roomy new porch better in keeping with the home's architectural style. Cedar shingles on the addition lend a period finish and blend with the main level's wood siding, a dramatic change from the former gray stucco walls. Nearby Arts and Crafts homes inspired the exterior color palette of Shaker red, moss green, yellow, and khaki. Concrete pavers made to look like stone replaced the front lawn for a finishing touch.

BY DESIGN
Avoid spindly leg syndrome

Columns supporting a two-story porch pose a special design challenge. If you are looking for a clean design, it's tempting to go with what is structurally sufficient. On a large porch, even a 6×6 may look spindly. From a structural point of view 4×4 or 4×6 posts could provide adequate support. But looks count too. Wrap the structural members with plywood or 1× to beef up the framing visually, lending a reassuring air of substance while helping to tie the porch to the house. Avoiding a cantilever, such as shown in the "before" photo *below*, can help too. Not everyone trusts the strength of an overhang.

before

Boost the scale

A gangly stairway, plain vanilla railings, and spindly supporting posts did this second-story porch no favors. Worst of all, it was on the lakefront side of a Georgia vacation home, where good looks count.

Homeowners Rick and Lisa McKay called in designer Craig Kettlers to reinvent the porch as part of a whole-house remodel. To improve the rear exterior aesthetically and structurally, Kettles added posts of a more substantial scale. He also extended the patio and replaced railings with a version of his own that incorporates metal bars. Green paint allows the house to blend with nature and keeps the maintenance low. "Light colors don't do well if they're near water because of potential mildew," Kettles says.

Cut back

As pleasant as a front porch might be, it tends to rob adjacent rooms of daylight. That was one reason the new owners of this former summer cottage decided to remake the front facade. The ever-so-slightly off-center front door also ruined the home's otherwise classic symmetry. So off came the porch (and the beach-stripe awnings), and on went a centered—and enlarged—entry with a flat-roofed portico. The updated look is far more elegant than the original, yet still in character for the 100-year-old house.

before

before

Meld old with new

Guest shouldn't be left standing in the rain, a good argument for every front door offering at least minimal protection from the elements. This porch does that and more, boosting its curb appeal by enhancing the storybook quality of the house. It offers several lessons on how to meld old with new. For starters, the metal roof echoes that of the bump-out bay window. The miniature window in the porch gable mimics the effect of brickwork in the gable of the house. The arch of the porch ceiling neatly responds to the curve of the roof. Finally, posts and fascia are exactly in scale with the house. The result: a porch that not only shelters but welcomes in high style.

The virtues of metal roofs

The vertical seams in metal roofs are a beautiful counterpoint to shingled roofs and complement the parallel structure of pergolas. Available in a wide array of colors, metal roofs are wind- and fire-resistant, energy-efficient, and lightweight, and have a lifespan ranging from 25 to 50 years.

before

Combine elements

The once drab and dysfunctional rear elevation of this Baltimore home takes on front-of-the house charm and renewed purpose thanks to a well-proportioned octagonal breakfast room and adjoining pergola-roofed porch. It's the stalwart posts of the pergola that give this porch presence and help it complement the home's 1927 English cottage style. The deck-like openness of the structure makes it a welcoming place to lounge, while a roof extending from the octagonal addition shelters the entryway.

Although the existing roof is capped with Vermont slate, homeowner and architect Ken Hart chose less-costly metal roofing for the bump-out. The green-and-blue-shaded metal roofing picks up on the slate's natural hues while introducing another texture.

Add a gable

In this home's previous incarnation, not only was the entryway obscured by foliage, it was upstaged by the balcony over the garage. As part of a whole-house renovation, the entry gained a new gabled portico porch approached by a graceful stairway. The portico melds with the balcony, giving the house a new unity. Most of the home's basic lines stayed intact, but detailing cured the stark appearance. The new porch clearly identifies the path of entry into the home, diverting unwarranted attention from the garage, which now recedes in the shade. The gray-and-white paint scheme elevates the home's look from ho-hum to quiet classic. Also elegant, the new railing style eliminates the deck-like look of the balcony.

before

Unbungle

A previous owner enclosed the porch on this bungalow to get additional living area. This "fix" masked the charm of the original design. The new owners wanted to preserve that charm but not at the expense of the additional square footage. The solution: Instead of getting rid of the discordant element, the new design tucked it behind an L-shape porch and pergola. The structure made way for period details that brought the entire home into harmony, including shaped rafter tails and columns cloned from the originals.

before

Transforming power

Brian and Emily Hammers of Medford, Oregon, discovered how to turn a dowdy home into a handsomely appointed bungalow. Their strategy? Look inward. "We wanted the outside of our house to reflect the interior's Craftsman style," Emily says. To achieve that, the couple topped off a whole-house renovation with an elegant front porch. A new tile-shingled roof features a wide gable that echoes the pitch of the main roof. Exposed rafters, in keeping with Craftsman bare-bones sensibility, open up the entryway.

before

before

Uncover hidden style

Kent and Sondra Carlson chose the worst house on one of Des Moines' most prestigious residential streets, spotting the potential in the great corner lot with nearly 300 feet of frontage. They also recognized the true personality of the 1920s home, with its gracious period details, including a low-pitch hipped roof and 3-foot-deep overhangs.

"The house had been Colonialized, but it was definitely an Arts and Crafts house," says Kent. The couple brought the home back to its roots by adding a pergola-covered wraparound porch. They also opted to delete the shutters as elements not in keeping with the style. The home's new meandering walkway completes the Arts and Crafts aesthetic.

before

Cheer up a blank look

Often, adding a porch completes your home's unfinished business. Despite many compelling features—deep eaves, interesting gables, and nice structural variation—this house greeted the world with a blank expression. The owners recognized that their home had its origins in the Craftsman and Prairie styles, both of which always have ample front porches. It was a natural next step to study the features of such porches and apply some good ideas to their own home. If you have a house without a porch or with a remuddled later addition, begin by exploring your home's architectural roots (see *chapter 2*). You're bound to find inspiration.

Look to the eaves

From the day Karen and Tim Conn moved into their Omaha home, they vowed it would someday have a proper front porch. Previous owners had tacked on an underscaled stoop with a metal roof—not what the Conns had in mind. Instead, they replaced the entry with a nearly full-width veranda designed to meld with the home's classic styling. "We exactly matched the original roof pitch, eaves, fascia, and lumber dimensions," Karen says.

The Conn family did almost all of the work themselves, recycling some materials. The children chiseled mortar from old bricks salvaged from a redo of their garage. Those bricks now form support posts for the porch's columns. And the same antique ornamental iron fencing that fronts the Conns' yard serves as their porch's balustrade. Period beaded-board covers the ceilings and overhangs, and fretwork brackets top the Craftsman-style posts.

before

Take it backward

This 1884 Elgin, Illinois, home suffered a "modernization" that replaced the original porch with a concrete-and-wrought-iron structure. Present owners Susan and Keith Farnham decided to undo those changes to bring back the home's gilded glory. The ironwork came down, and a new porch was built right over the old concrete pad. The revamped design brings the family outside. "Porches get you out of the house," Keith says, "and then you become part of the neighborhood." The Farnhams made sure the new scheme was built in compliance with guidelines set by the local historical society. They painted the home in a seven-color scheme: dark green for the floor, a light blue ceiling, pink siding, beige trim, purple rails, dark blue under the eaves, and gold details on the spindles and columns. The gold is automotive paint that has a slight sheen to it.

TAKE AWAY

3 tips to remember

1 Echo the roofline to help your porch "fit in."

2 Remove fascia to expose rafter ends, adding architecutral detail.

3 Tame landscaping growth to open up the views of your porch.

before

Echo the roofline

When Joel Mack and Barbara Borden bought their Coronado, California, home, it lacked strong connections with the outdoors and an entry to welcome visitors. Built before 1910, the house once had an open front porch, but previous owners enclosed it to create a sunroom. With two kids, Joel and Barbara needed all of the interior square footage they could get, so they didn't re-open the porch. Instead, they built a small covered front porch that extends forward into the yard, but that falls within the city's zoning requirements by just a few inches. The hip roof and exposed rafter tails of the simple porch help tie it to the home's Craftsman origins.

styles

Whether your house is 10 or 110 years old, its look is based on a distinct architectural style. Knowing your home's **ARCHITECTURAL HERITAGE** gives you a valuable sense of direction as you plan your new porch. For example, this **CRAFTSMAN-STYLE PORCH** is awash with great architectural detail that the porch puts to good use. The tapered columns, Shingle-style surface, barrel-style ceiling, and style-specific light fixture all echo the hallmarks of Craftsman style. You may need to look hard to tease out the latent style of your house, especially if you own a suburban **BUILDER'S SPECIAL**. But uncover its architectural roots and you'll gain insights on what elements to pull into a porch. On the following pages are houses representing some predominant American home styles, each with a stunning porch that gets it right.

Colonial

The hallmark of the Colonial style is a no-nonsense rectangular profile, a result of post-and-beam framing. Oddly enough, most early Colonial homes had no porch at all, relying instead on the scant shelter provided by a cantilevered second story.

These one- and two-story designs featured elements borrowed from modest English houses of the 17th century: tall peaked roofs (some hipped), shallow eaves (or no eaves at all), and little decorative molding. Unlike its English forebears, a Colonial was usually made entirely of wood, a material in short supply in the mother country.

A blank canvas

It wasn't long before the style became a blank canvas for elegant elaboration, aided by carpenter's

handbooks of the time that showed how to make more and more elaborate doorways and cornices. Slowly, it became the style we know today, with a front door flanked by decorative pilasters and housed under a gabled portico. Doorway treatments became more elaborate too, with semi-circular or elliptical fanlights, and sidelights beside the door. Layered cornices under the eaves and above windows include dentils and other decorative elements. Iron handrails were a staple, often curving outward to match the sweep of the porch stairs.

Later variations were built of brick, with classically styled trim and dormers.

Eventually, the practical advantage of the porch won out. Porches expanded on Colonial-style homes, some rising two stories. Majestic columns supported the porch roof, and sometimes a second-story balcony as well. Some, including Dutch Colonials, gained full-width porches, anticipating the "living" porch so popular as sheltered workspaces on farmhouses (see *page 60*). The French Colonial went a step further, adding deep two-level porches that shaded interior space built tall to maximize airflow. The style came into full bloom with the Early Classical Revival style where a porch was almost always part of the package, often matching the full height of the house and dramatically highlighting the entryway.

Modern variations

The modern Colonial home is popular with homeowners because of its handsome dignity and American heritage. Builders like it because it is simple to build. The style's classic quality carries a sense of enduring value, and a porch adds an aspect of welcoming warmth. Most modern Colonials fairly cry out for a porch addition, and benefit from details such as columns, dentils, layered molding, and iron railings.

OPPOSITE: The regal porch on this beautiful Colonial is a long way from the utilitarian origins of the style. It clearly marks the entryway, pulling together the upper and lower stories, including a faux balcony that frames a Palladian window.

Colonial

Colonial elaboration

Although its origins were plain and utilitarian, as America prospered the Colonial style added Georgian features. The arch in its many forms— whether a fanlight, a cornice, or the curve of a portico ceiling—quickly caught on and is a handy way to add architectural interest. Fascia grew more elaborate.

Also over time, banks of multipane windows became increasingly common on Colonial homes. The small panes were a matter of necessity; the only way to make panes was to blow bottle shapes and slice them into small rectangles. The charm of the resulting window is magnetic—well worth adding if your porch will have windows on its windy side or if you choose to fill a gable with bold latticework. Remember that adding a porch will heighten awareness of windows that are enclosed by, or adjacent to, your new space.

ABOVE: If styled correctly, a pergola extension suits the Colonial style, especially when coupled with a crisp portico. The result: an entranceway that extends a stylish welcome and adds some partially shaded outdoor living space.

RIGHT: A grid in the gable of this Colonial porch matches the multipaned windows.

OPPOSITE: If your budget is tight, you can achieve a fanlight effect over an entry door with the creative use of trim.

Colonial

Colonial full-facade porches

We can thank settlers in the Louisiana Territory for adding an expansive one-story front porch to Colonial homes. Sometimes known as "living" porches, they were built so household chores could be done outdoors with the benefit of cooling breezes—the better to cope with the heat and humidity of the lower Mississippi. (The living porch was a great idea that grew in popularity, becoming a key element of the Farmhouse style—see *pages 58–62*.) Offering a place to relax in the evening was an added benefit. Some living porches had high ceilings, the better to promote air circulation and, when the track of the sun was lower in the wintertime, increase interior light. The style continues to delight to this day as a folksier take on a classic style.

ABOVE: The roof on this porch overlaps the second story to create high-ceiling drama and plenty of airflow.

RIGHT: Stonework is a great way to anchor a porch, especially when the porch extends to include an open patio area.

OPPOSITE: Incorporating a portico in a porch emphasizes the entryway in grand style. If you are concerned that your new porch will shade the interior of your home, take a cue from this approach and add tall windows or a secondary entry with windowed double doors.

3 ways to make a Colonial porch

1 Use a gabled portico to highlight your entryway.

2 Add rich, multilayered fascia.

3 Incorporate an arch in the portico ceiling, fanlight, or cornice.

Farmhouse

By the early part of the 19th century, anything English had fallen out of vogue, especially the Colonial style with its roots in Georgian architecture.

Instead, American home builders looked to Italy (and found the Italianate style), greater Europe (Gothic Revival), and especially Greece (Greek Revival), the wellspring of democracy and great architecture.

Equipped with pattern books such as Andrew Jackson Downing's *Cottage Residences* published in 1842, homeowners had a whole new world of styles to choose from (including the Swiss, Oriental, and Egyptian styles that never quite gained traction).

Lumped together, these types comprise a style we know best as expressed in the thousands of farmhouses spread across the American Midwest. With the Farmhouse style, the front porch had taken hold. No country home could be without one. The porch had become more than an architectural element, it represented a way of life that spanned the warmth and security of indoor time and the shaded fresh air of outdoors, essential for comfort in an era before air-conditioning. Here are some of the particulars:

Italianate

Italianate homes (see the *bottom of page 60*) often have a hipped roof with a porch following suit. Porch posts are ornate and often joined by a flat arch. The porches range from none at all to wraparound types, but are always limited to one story. Porch eaves have elaborate brackets, mimicking those of the house.

Greek Revival

Of the Romantic styles, Greek Revival (*opposite*) was the most popular—so universal that it became known as the "National" style. Part of its popularity was political—Americans felt great sympathy for the Greek war of independence. But the style also offered dignity and a touch of grandeur to a domestic abode, and was seldom without a "living" porch across the facade or along a wing. Front doors often have a transom and sidelights, but never fanlights. Easily constructed square columns are common, though upscale versions might also have round columns.

Gothic Revival

The Gothic Revival style (see *below*), familiar to us

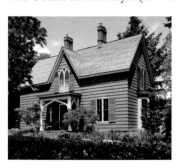

through Grant Wood's iconic *American Gothic* painting, has high-pitched roofs with gables centered in the front of the house. To contrast this, porch roofs are low profile but have elaborate flat arches and brackets between the square posts.

OPPOSITE: The unadorned utility of the simple wing porch on this Greek Revival can be traced right back to the classic elegance of the Parthenon.

4 ways to make a Farmhouse porch

1 Make your porch an ample "living" porch.

2 Play up Italianate, Gothic Revival, or Greek Revival elements in your home.

3 Keep ornaments minimal to be true to the style's character.

4 Consider the expansiveness of a wraparound porch.

Farmhouse

The "living" porch

An element borrowed from warm-climate Colonial porches, the expansive living porch is a functional Farmhouse feature. Sheltered from sun and summer cloudburst alike, the living porch was an indispensable spot for shelling peas, ironing, mending—any domestic chore that could be taken outdoors. It was transitional space, half indoors and half outdoors, that melded the house with its surroundings. In the evenings, it was the perfect place to sit in a rocker and watch the sun go down.

That's the aspect we love about it today—it is a generous space in which to lounge or entertain. Whether fronting a wing of the house, running along the full-front facade, or wrapping around a corner, it provides an outdoor escape and a handy way of adding some style with its elegant columns, railings, and welcoming stairs.

ABOVE: A wraparound porch gives a spacious base to a house as vertical as the prairie is flat. The result: pure Americana.

RIGHT: Extra detailing on the post bases of the new porch is all that is needed to echo under-eave brackets on this Italianate house.

OPPOSITE: Even new homes in the Farmhouse tradition benefit from a porch. This one uses an extended landing to pull together disparate elements like the bumpout bay and the sheltering overhang.

Victorian

Balloon framing has been around since the early 19th century, but really hit its stride in the Victorian Era (1860–1900). The framing method used 2×4s instead of cumbersome posts and beams.

This method allowed builders to add elements that would otherwise have been difficult to build—things like turrets, towers, multiple stories of varied sizes, and elaborate porches. All had elaborate architectural details.

Decoration abounds

Architectural embellishment was proof of the young nation's prosperity, just as in Great Britain it showed off the economic power of the British

Empire. In America, even a laborer's house might get fanciful trim along the porch eaves or delicately carved brackets at the porch posts, thanks not in small part to vast timber resources and the mass production of a wide range of architectural elements. Cladding included lap siding, crisscrossing flatwork, and shingles, plenty of shingles—square, fish scale, octagonal, teardrop, diamond, and diagonal—used to decorate the

steep gables and dormers. A blank wall was a thing to be shunned, leading to half-timber beams and stucco where there was no siding or shingles. Porches received special treatment with delicate spindle work and brackets between the posts, elaborate friezes, and curved or turned railing balusters.

Queen Anne

The Queen Anne style is one of the easiest Victorian styles to recognize, with its many gables, a turret or two, fretwork boards along the eaves, gingerbread trim, and fabulous color combinations. It is the style we most associate

with the Victorian era. The Queen Anne style hosts just about every configuration of porch imaginable— two-story, entrance-only, full-width— but is perhaps best known for the wraparound porch. The typically low-profile hip roof often has gable or turreted add-ons. It always has some element that highlights the entryway, like the gable roof directional. Posts might be doubled, or even quadrupled, and are typically turned. Wraparounds often had two entrances: a grand one for welcoming guests and another to connect the porch to a parlor or dining room.

OPPOSITE: In addition to its turned balusters and posts, this Victorian porch adds a gable with fish-scale shingles and even a touch of metal roofing. Because the style incorporates so much variety, modern touches, such as the skylights on the porch, fit right in.

4 ways to make a Victorian porch

1 Choose a roof element to highlight your entryway.

2 Add turned posts of adequate scale.

3 Mimic details found elsewhere on the house.

4 Consider adding a second entrance to the porch.

Victorian

Victorian detailing

All the brackets, turned posts, and spindle work may look like architectural detailing run amok, but there is method to the madness. For example, the dentiling along the porch fascia in the photo *below* is kept subtle so it doesn't fight with brackets along the second-story frieze. Even the elaborately lacey vergeboard on the gables of the house *at right* is left to carry the day without introducing other fancy work that would detract from it.

It is not just filigree that makes a Victorian; in fact, some Victorian homes are remarkably free of detailed ornamentation. Multiple rooflines and a sense of balanced asymmetry also mark the style. Gables abound on most Victorian houses; adding one to a porch is a natural way to tie new to old. Deep eaves and layered fascia treatments are other common features well worth imitating when adding a porch to a Victorian home.

ABOVE: With plenty of lacey vergeboard under the eaves, elaborate spindle work on the porch eaves would be too much of a good thing. Simple post brackets add just enough detail.

RIGHT: The rounded sweep of a wraparound porch calls for a talented contractor, but the trouble is well worth it.

OPPOSITE: The trick of building a Queen Anne porch is adding period details without the elements fighting one another. This porch keeps things in balance with the emphasis on creating an ideal place to sit in a rocker and watch the world go by.

Victorian

Mimicking roof lines

The Queen Anne style has vitality beyond its detailed trim; it also beautifully combines a multitude of rooflines. This offers plenty of options for planning the roofline of a new porch. Often a small gable roof can mark the entryway, but not when it might fight with other gables already in place. The angle of the gable doesn't have to exactly match those that are already on the house, but should vary enough to look intentional. A flat roof or low-profile hipped roof is a good tactic when too much is going on. An open gable with decorative stickwork keeps things light while adding architectural detail. Roofing materials can vary too, though it is usually best to pick up on something already used on the house. Queen Annes might have as many as three different roofing materials, so there is often plenty to choose from.

ABOVE: This porch surrounds the base of a turret, with an extra-heavy spindle-work frieze to give it presence.

LEFT: A new home achieves the Victorian profile without all the labor-intensive details and custom woodworking. Adding a gable to the porch and incorporating turned posts and some gingerbread trim does the trick.

OPPOSITE: Perching a balcony on the roof adds a lovely new dimension to a porch and an enticing addition to a bedroom.

Shingle

As the style of choice for late-19th-century vacation homes, Shingle-style houses are a free-spirited variation on the Victorian theme. True to its name, the style's predominant characteristic is wood shingle cladding.

But it almost always has a predominant front porch, a feature that plays an important role in pulling together the many elements of the style. This uniquely American style remains popular

today, not least of all for its casual dignity, its ability to pull together so many varied elements—and its welcoming porches. A characteristic of the style's homes and porches is the conspicuous use of natural materials. Foundations are often stone or stone veneered. And the shingle or clapboard siding is often stained or painted in the rustic tones of nature.

Shingle-style porches are often placed asymmetrically. They come with square or round columns, though true to this free-form style the columns may also be shingled or built of stone. Like the windows, doors, and cornices of Shingle-style homes, porch decoration is minimal, extending to little more that a slight arch between the columns.

Variety overhead

Where the style really cuts loose is in its roof profile. Most any kind of roof can top off a Shingle-style home—the barnlike gambrel roof, two gables meeting at an angle, a hipped roof, or a conical turret. Often more than one type of roofing

material is used. Shingle-style porches usually echo some unique element of the roofline, helping to unify the look. Sometimes the roof seems to embrace the porch, fully integrating it into the house.

Shingle homes originated along the ocean shores of the northeastern states. When built within sight of the sea, a Shingle-style home might

include a "widow's walk"—a porchlike rooftop aerie for viewing the ocean. Although Shingle-style porches are never more than one story, the widow's walk inspired adding a balcony above the porch. The balcony provides an opportunity for decoration and is a handsome, transforming feature.

OPPOSITE: A porch arbor on this grand Shingle-style home suits the style's ability to pull together varied elements. The arbor emphasizes the entryway while hosting climbing vines that have a softening effect on the look of the house.

TAKE AWAY

3 ways to make a Shingle porch

1 Incorporate shingles into the columns or knee wall.

2 Keep the look casual with a relaxed, comfortable air.

3 Introduce a new roof profile.

Shingle

Shingle style as retreat

People still love the Shingle style's rustic, get-away-from-it-all feel. The concept of home as a retreat makes this vacation-oriented style universally appealing. Modern interpretations of the style abound, almost always with a well-appointed porch whose crisp detailing has a lot to do with giving it a sophisticated edge. And it can dress up a bit. Although asymmetry is one of its common characteristics, the Shingle style is just varied enough to embrace dead-center symmetry as well. Finally, because vacation homes have a distinct sense of place, the style is made to fit in well with its surroundings, often by means of the front porch. Its rustic personality can make even a suburban cul-de-sac appear woodsy.

ABOVE: While two-story porches are rare in the Shingle style, if you have a lakeside view like this place, a double-decker makes a lot of sense—another example of the style's flexibility.

RIGHT: Arches are a common feature, whether incorporated into the porch or over a balcony. Stone is also a common ingredient in a Shingle-style porch, a reminder of its coastal origins.

OPPOSITE: In the tradition of the widow's walk, a balcony railing is a fine addition to a simple porch.

Craftsman

The Craftsman style emerged from California in the early 1900s, influenced by the English Arts and Crafts movement as well as the meticulous joinery of Asian architecture. It quickly grew into a uniquely American style, giving birth to the bungalow,

a Craftsman icon that almost always has a generous porch. Crafty detailing on these porches includes shaped rafter ends and supportive corbels. Open gables on porches show off stickwork—the trusslike rafter supports. Stone or brick piers that support the porch columns are a hallmark of the Craftsman style. They run from grade level to above the floor. More often than not the wooden columns they support are tapered.

A love of craftsmanship

The Craftsman style avoids anything that looks

shoddy or mass produced, instead seeking out the rough-hewn beauty found in traditional crafts. If the imprint of the hammer shows in ironwork or the mark of the plane is evident in a door's finish, all the better. The extravagant display of Victorian detailing was consciously avoided—after all, Craftsman homes were originally built to suit a laborer's budget.

Instead, a wide range of materials adds interest and variety. Whether stone, brick, clapboard, shingles, concrete block, or stucco, the materials are left unadorned—the better to prove they are handmade, not churned out by a machine.

The color scheme of a Craftsman-style home is subdued and cued to the warm hues of nature.

This helps the porch and house blend well with the surrounding landscape and complements the colors of wood and stone.

Those features set the Craftsman style apart. It is not just final appearance that matters, but what the porch is made of and the skill with which it is put together. As such, it is almost a state of mind. Born of a social movement that asserted that great design should be within the reach of every homeowner, the style conjures up notions of timelessness, integrity, honest work—great values on which to build a home.

That's why the style has so much appeal today, morphing into thousands of variations that echo original Craftsman elements. Here and on the following pages are Craftsman porches, as well as Craftsman-influenced porches, all of which incorporate aspects of this versatile style. With each example, the final effect is warm and welcoming: a porch that says you're home.

OPPOSITE: Many Craftsman porches boast an open gable with thick beams that signal permanence.

3 ways to make a Craftsman porch

1 Feature posts with a stone or brick base and a tapered wood column.

2 Add interest with brackets and exposed rafters.

3 Choose simple, rough-hewn materials.

Craftsman

Craftsman adaptability

Although the humble bungalow *below* is famously associated with the Craftsman style, it was too good a thing not to be applied to larger homes. Two-story versions increasingly appeared as the style swept across the United States. Each had an ample front porch—a feature no Craftsman house can do without. But as the style stretched beyond the one-story bungalow, the porch stretched too—see the two-level example *opposite*. Yet the elements remain the same. The tapered columns are there, set on masonry pedestals that run from grade level to the second story. No fascia hides the rafters at the edge of a low-pitch hipped roof. The look remains undisputedly Craftsman.

ABOVE: Stone bases reflect the Craftsman appreciation of natural materials. Craftsman homes often have triptych windows. In this case, French doors replace two windows for ready access to the front porch.

RIGHT: Hipped roofs are common to Craftsman homes, sometimes taking on a fanciful cottage look.

Although stacked porches are not a common feature on Craftsman houses, the style can certainly stretch to accommodate them. In this case, the second story was achieved by extending the column bases before making the transition to tapered columns.

Craftsman

Craftsman columns

Whether it is doubled, tapered, or bracketed, a Craftsman porch support has two parts: the pedestal below and the column above. The pedestal might be brick or stone or part of a wood-clad balustrade, but it typically reaches to grade level. On occasion, the columns are doubled, or even quadrupled. Whatever the variation, the Craftsman look always seems to be grounded, sturdily settled into its environment. The final profile is one of substance—anything but spindly—almost as if the house was designed to withstand anything the elements could throw at it. A style designed for those of humble means, its columns offered Everyman a grand entrance.

ABOVE: Deep eaves and a high gable lend drama to the porch entryway of this Craftsman-influenced new home. Even nontraditional materials like the aluminum soffits used here don't stand in the way of the style.

LEFT: Beefy corbels overlapping the porch posts give a unified, distinctly Craftsman look to this house.

OPPOSITE: An appreciation of the manual arts has always been part of the Craftsman tradition, something very noticeable in this porch's folksy stonework.

Prairie

In addition to its low-profile hipped roof and overall rectangularity, a Prairie-style home is recognizable by its large front porch, typically centered on the front facade of the house.

Often the porch roof echoes a dominant dormer, also centered on the house. Like the house roof, the eaves of the porch roof are deep, with a pronounced overhang suitable for protecting the

house from all that Midwest weather can throw at it. At its heart, the Prairie style is substantial, with nothing frivolous about it.

Unlike Craftsman columns, Prairie-style columns are seldom tapered and sometimes of one piece. Often they are made of brick or stucco and may have a touch of geometric or botanical decoration, touches Louis Sullivan, the second most famous architect associated with the style, pushed to perfection. Many Prairie-style porches included banks of double-hung windows, a way of getting three seasons of use from a porch

and keeping the snow out in the winter. The ornamentation is simple or nonexistent, without brackets or arches. Railings are straightforward,

usually using square wood balusters. Open porches often have wide stairways that pour onto landings or patio areas. Long stone or brick walls flank some Prairie-style stairways. The walls may be topped by wide planters or urns, a great way to help tie the porch to the landscape.

A Prairie-style porch suits fierce summers well because of its spaciousness and the generous shade produced by the overhang of the eaves. These porches take in a full view of the neighborhood

and comfortably accommodate a large number of people. Many homes also had sleeping porches on the back or side of the house, the only way to beat the heat before the advent of air-conditioning. Today, those porches are a way to combine a degree of privacy with outdoor living. Like all great porches, the Prairie-style porch is functional, friendly, and good-looking.

OPPOSITE: The Four-Square is a folk style closely related to the Prairie style. Four-Square homes often have full-width porches with base and post treatments in the Prairie tradition.

TAKE AWAY

4 ways to make a Prairie porch

1 Use wide steps to achieve a horizontal look.

2 Keep the porch to one story.

3 Avoid decorative arches and brackets.

4 Add deep eaves to offer protection from the sun.

design

Design is all about merging architectural vision and budget considerations with your objectives for how you'll use your porch. Even if you plan to **ENLIST A DESIGN-BUILDER OR ARCHITECT** to do the heavy lifting on the design of your porch, launching the process with some creativity of your own is bound to save false steps. Your participation may be as light as marking favorite porches in this book or making a collection of magazine clippings. Or it may be as involved as **ASSEMBLING A SCALE MODEL OF YOUR HOUSE** and trying out a bunch of miniature porch options. As long as you've clarified what you want (and what you don't want), you'll give the pros a running start on delivering a porch that's everything you hoped for. Here are some **DOWN-TO-EARTH METHODS** for designing a porch that is right for you.

Porch possibilities

Porch planning travels on two tracks at once—the aesthetic and the practical. In a best-case scenario, form won't get in the way of function and vice versa.

In fact, sometimes the pursuit of a great look (extra-wide steps, for example) can lead to something surprisingly useful (a stairway that provides comfortable overflow seating for a party).

A porch can enhance your life more than you may expect, so before you get down to the construction details and budget, make a wish list. Consider some of the things a porch can do for you, then design with an eye toward maximizing those benefits. Here are a few of the things a new porch has to offer:

• **The casual ambience of a porch** is the perfect setting for conversation. Many homeowners speak of wanting their porch to convey that they are welcoming and enjoy being in touch with their neighborhood. If sociability is important to you, be sure to provide ample space for comfortable seating.

• **Diners seem to linger longer** on a porch. If you plan to "eat out" a lot, be sure your porch can accommodate an adequately sized dining table with chairs, or occasional tables next to chairs. Also check that the eating area won't be a bottleneck. Insects love food, so screening in the eating area, if not the whole porch, should be part of your planning. Is a grilling area possible? An outdoor kitchen?

Porch dining is one of the delights of summer. Plan not just for the table and chairs, but also for room to push back each chair for easy access. Also make sure a pathway remains to walk past the table.

• **A porch provides a buffer zone** that helps maintain order in the house, a sheltered place to remove and store muddy boots, sports equipment, and large toys that would be difficult to store inside. If this is your goal, consider an area with knee walls, rather than a railing, to hide things from view— maybe even some built-in storage.

• **A porch extends the time** you can enjoy the outdoors. Screened porches make twilight and evening gatherings possible. If you install storm-and-screen type windows, perhaps coupled with a heat source, the porch will be usable most or even all of the year.

• **A shady porch** open to breezes offers relief on hot summer days without switching on the air-conditioner. An overhead fan dials up the cool. The shelter provided by a porch roof can also cool the interior of your home.

• **A sunny porch** can enhance your gardening life. If you incorporate overhead window panels or add skylights, you can exercise your green thumb during cold months by bringing selected potted plants onto the porch. You can also jump-start your summer garden by starting seeds a month or so earlier than you would outdoors.

LEFT: Open to breezes supplemented by overhead fans, a porch is one cool place in the summertime. Interior rooms benefit, too: The added shade provided by the porch roof helps limit the use of air-conditioning.

BELOW: A small potting area is an attractive and useful addition to a porch. Sheltered areas are sometimes warm enough to give outdoor plants an early start.

The planning process

A porch is a major project. The more time you invest in making detailed plans, the happier you'll be with the result.

The following pages show how to start with simple drawings and models to prepare for the more elaborate and sophisticated plans that will satisfy a building inspector and guide a builder. Begin with deciding how you will use the porch, and create initial plans that ensure it will meet your needs. Let these initial decisions and desires guide you as you move on to the final plans.

While a deck is a relatively simple thing to construct, a porch has all the complexity of a miniature house. In fact, most municipal codes are based on the idea that a porch might someday be enclosed and made into living space. That is why there are stringent structural requirements and why the final plans will almost certainly need to be generated by an architect or a design-builder, and all the more reason why you should bring to the table a clear idea of what you want.

Sometimes the ideal is just not possible and some compromise will be called for. For instance, allowing overly generous space for dining and lounging may lead to a porch that overwhelms the house. Conversely, a certain combination of arches and columns might look great, but obstruct views. Clearly, making such compromises is easier well before construction begins.

Brainstorming

Imitation is the sincerest form of flattery; it is also an effective design strategy. Bookmark appealing photos in this book, clip photos from magazines, and do a web search of porch images. If you want to take photos of appealing porches in your area, ask permission first. Not only is it simple courtesy, but the ensuing conversation could provide useful information about what the owners like about their porch, what aspects they would change, and how they managed the process of getting it built.

Check out chapters 4 and 5 to acquaint yourself with some of the possibilities for materials and structural requirements. Do some Internet exploring. If you want to incorporate posts or columns, type "architectural columns" into your search engine and you'll find many companies with a wide variety of options to choose from. A search for "porch railings" will yield a similar cornucopia.

Sizing and shaping to meet your needs

Once you have a good idea of how you want to use your porch, think about the size and shape that will meet those needs comfortably. You'll need room not only for the furniture you plan to use, but also for pathways so people can comfortably walk through and into the house.

Rough out the plan

Using graph paper or a clear graph ruler, make a drawing showing where you want things to be. The drawing can be rough, but it should be to scale—for instance, ¼ or ½ inch to 1 foot.

If you'd like to experiment with a variety of arrangements, use graph paper to draw a basic floor plan, indicating the entry door and any secondary doors, windows, and any obstructions like posts or columns that might block a view. Next, make scale cutouts that represent furnishings, planters, and even area rugs. Be sure to leave room for ample pathways. If you plan a large porch, consider groupings that seat six people—about the maximum number for comfortable conversation.

A real-life test

Clear an area on your driveway. Use blue painter's tape to mark the dimensions of the porch and to indicate doors, windows, stairways, and posts. Use your outdoor furniture and any easily toted indoor items to stand in for the furnishings you'll use on your porch. Give the arrangement a test drive. Pull out a chair and sit at the table. Walk around to see that there will be no uncomfortable traffic bottlenecks. Consider light sources, including permanent fixtures as well as table and floor lamps.

WHAT IT TAKES

Steps to create extra seating

Deep stairs double as overflow seating for social occasions. To make them more comfortable, plan for the steps to be at least 4 feet wide, so someone can walk past two seated people. Make the stair treads 16 to 20 inches deep (as opposed to the usual 12 inches), enough room for someone to lean back comfortably.

Choosing a roof configuration

Without a roof, a porch is but a deck. A porch roof needs to look as if it has always been there, a natural complement to your home's profile. In many cases, it sets the tone for the porch because it is so visible to passersby. It also has much to do with the overall cost of the project.

See *chapter 4* to learn some of the ways roofs are constructed. If you have a two-story house, the porch's roof will likely meet against the house's siding. On a one-story house, the porch's roof will tie into the house's roof.

These pages show the five most common roof shapes. Linking a porch roof with a home is seldom simple; too often the location of windows and the very shape of the house complicate things. As a result, a porch roof may have to be a combination of two or more of these shapes to get the job done.

• **A "flat roof"** actually slopes slightly away from the house for drainage, at a rate of about ¼ inch per running foot. Building a flat roof calls for larger-than-usual joists and beams, since it must support snow in the winter, and uses special rolled roofing materials rather than shingles.

A flat roof may be constructed to make an upper-story deck, which in turn may or may not be roofed. The flat deck will be built on top of the (slightly sloping) roof. Special gutter systems have been developed to direct water that runs through the decking to gutters around the roof.

Flat roof

Hip roof

Gable roof

Turret or gazebo roof

Shed roof

• **A hip roof** is complicated to build, requiring framing with compound miters that are time-consuming to measure and cut. But if your home has a hip roof or hip roof sections, a hip roof can be the most attractive option for your porch.

• **A gable roof has two sides** that slope upward to meet at a top ridge in the middle, so it presents a triangular shape when viewed from the front. It's a bit complicated to frame and will be more expensive than a shed roof. A gable porch roof is often the only logical and attractive choice, since it can repeat rooflines found elsewhere on the house.

However, in some cases it is not possible to install a gable roof. If there is a second-story window or other obstruction above a first-story porch, a gable roof's peak may bump into it, or come too close to bumping into it to look right. In that case, you may need to lower the slope of the gable roof, or install a shed roof instead.

• **A turret or gazebo roof** is a bravura touch that radically alters the look of a house. Framing one is mighty complicated, as is trimming it out and roofing it. Some homeowners opt for incorporating a manufactured ready-to-assemble sunroom product, with clear acrylic or glass panels. Because the height of the roof increases with its floor area, a gazebo porch (or section of a porch) is usually fairly small.

• **A shed roof** is a simple flat surface that angles downward from the house. This is often the least expensive way to go, because it uses minimal materials. In addition, the builder needs to make no complicated angle cuts for the rafters, and installing roofing, flashing, and gutters is straightforward.

The name "shed" conjures a shacklike appearance, and a shed roof can indeed look tacked-on in certain situations. However, an outwardly sloping roof can add welcome complexity to a home's exterior lines. If its fascia is wrapped with matching trim, a shed roof will look like it belongs. And if a porch runs longer than 24 feet along the side of a house, a shed roof may be the only practical option.

WHAT IT TAKES
Capture the roof slope

To find your house's roof slope, hold a combination square against a long ruler as shown. Slide it until it lines up with the 12-inch mark on the ruler. Using the siding as a guide for keeping the rig level, line up the end of the ruler with the roof edge. (You may need to substitute a level for the ruler if you don't have horizontal siding.) Note the measurement on the combination square. For instance, if you read 4 inches on the combination square, the slope is 4:12. (For more on roof slope, see *page 109*.)

Envisioning

If you hire an architect or a good design-builder, you will receive drawings and perhaps also some high-tech ways to view your future porch in 3-D. But to get started, here are some good envisioning techniques you can employ yourself.

Imitation

If a neighbor has a porch that appeals to you, a good design-builder will be able to emulate it while adding touches that make yours unique. Take careful measurements, not only of the porch's basic dimensions, but also of the trim pieces, fascia, and posts. Note any ways in which the location of doors and windows differ from your own house. Codes may have tightened since your neighbor built the porch, so you may need to build the structure differently. With permission, take photographs of the interior and exterior of the porch.

Trace a photo

Many architects and designers use this method as a brainstorming tool. Take photos of your house from various angles. Choose vantage points that represent how people will most often view the porch. Make one or more large prints of two or more photos. (Hint: Digitally saturate the color to make the image more visible through tracing paper.) Tape tracing paper onto the print and start sketching. Try a bunch of approaches. Once you've found a design you like, trace over the pencil lines with a felt-tipped marker.

Measuring

Most architects and design-builders have CAD (computer aided design) programs that can pretty quickly produce drawings suitable for presenting to the building department. You can get involved (and save money) by providing the exact measurements of your house. Begin with a very rough drawing. Its sole function is to show what measurements go where. Include windows and doors and the height of the foundation and any slope to the grade, as well as dominant trim and fascia details.

Mount the drawing on a clipboard and start measuring. Measure the exact locations of windows and doors, as well as the slope of any rooflines. Working on graph paper or with a clear lined graph ruler, use a scale of ¼ inch to 1 foot or ½ inch to 1 foot to make an elevation drawing—a direct side view—of your house. Tape a piece of tracing paper over the drawing and make test drawings of your proposed porch. Make at least one more elevation drawing from another side of the porch. If your yard slopes significantly (see "Measuring yard slope," *opposite*), take that into account; the front of the porch may have a large space under its floor that will have to be filled in with skirting.

"A slope that varies by even 2 in 12 may not be noticeable by most people," notes architect Amy B. Reineri.

OPPOSITE: Sketching over a straight-on photo of the front of your house is similar to what architects call an elevation view. It will help you explore the best-looking roof slope, column mass, stair size, and overall size and silhouette.

LEFT: A plat survey is invaluable for determining setbacks and property lines, but double-check the measurements of your house.

WHAT IT TAKES
Measuring yard slope

If the yard where the porch will go is fairly level, you can skip this step. But if it slopes away significantly, its front will be raised high above the ground, meaning that you will need to install tall skirting (wood or masonry) to fill the space below the floor and perhaps a long stairway. Lay a level atop a straight 2×4 that is as long as the porch will be. Rest one end of the board where the slope begins. Measure between the top of the board and the ground every 3 feet to capture the shape and the extent of the slope.

Also make an overhead drawing, called a plan view. If you already have a survey, assessment, or other drawing of your house, use that to start with, but measure the house yourself to confirm the accuracy of the drawing. You don't have to draw the entire house, just a bird's-eye view of the portion where the porch will go. Draw the proposed porch, attached to the house.

Should you match nearby roof slopes? Generally, you are on safe ground if the porch roof has the same slope as that of your house's roof. But don't hesitate to vary it a bit if necessary.

"A slope that varies by even 2 in 12 may not be noticeable by most people," notes architect Amy B. Reineri of Casa Architecture in Hampton Roads, Virginia. "As an architect, I will see it, but it really doesn't bother the customers."

Often a difference in slope is not obvious even on an elevation drawing; once the porch is built, the difference is even less apparent. And if you build a shed roof on a house with gable roofs, a difference in slope usually doesn't matter at all.

CAD programs

If you have the inclination, you can purchase a CAD (computer aided design) program and use it to design your porch. A CAD program produces clear drawings and generates a list of materials—a real time-saver in itself. Inexpensive CADs render 2-D drawings; fancier versions produce 3-D drawings and let you "fly" around the porch to view it from most any angle.

However, if you are not already proficient in using a CAD, it's probably not worth your time to learn how to use a program like this. And these programs have limitations: There are likely only a few types of railing balusters, for instance, and probably not the exact style you want. Also, drawing curved lines is surprisingly difficult in most CAD programs.

A design-builder will likely have software that produces fairly realistic images of your house and a proposed porch. Plantings and other elements can be added, and the fly-around feature gives you a good look from many angles. It may take the designer some hours to construct the images, but once it's built he can quickly make major or minor changes as you look at the screen together. Not everyone uses CAD. Some designers shy away from such software because it takes too much time to make the initial construction.

Modeling

A scale model provides perhaps the ultimate 3-D image and is a great way to try on different porch options. Foam core, also known as paper-faced foam board, is a rigid, easy-to-cut material ideal for model making. Some types are printed with a ½-inch grid that simplifies transferring measurements to the board and aids in making accurate cuts. To make a model, have on hand the foam-core board, super glue, white glue, a self-healing mat for cutting, a utility knife and new blades, a clear graph ruler, a metal ruler, a pencil, and blue painter's tape or a black marker.

This approach begins with a model of your house, made to ¼-inch to ½-inch scale. After measuring your house and making a rough sketch, use a clear graph ruler and a pencil to mark the components. Use a utility knife and a metal ruler to cut them out. Be careful to hold the blade straight vertically as you cut so the edge of the piece will be square. Use blue painter's tape or a black marker to indicate windows and doors. You may also want to mark the foundation, particularly if it is elevated.

Super glue with a brush applicator quickly joins the sections and may be the only adhesive you need. (However, white glue may prove handy for gluing foam edge to foam edge—as when making a model pergola, for example.) Assemble the house model, including elements that may not connect to the porch but that will have an effect on the overall look.

Now the fun begins. Build several porch options so you can try them out. Build elements in sections, if possible. For example, a full porch with a shed roof can be broken into thirds. That way, you can see the effect of a small shed roof over the entryway, or a porch running two-thirds of the way across the front of your house, or a full-width porch. A small gable roof makes a worthwhile add-on. Capturing the size and shape of a gable on a sloped roof is challenging. Fold a scrap of paper and trim it with a scissors until you get the gable you want. Then use the scrap as a template for cutting the foam core.

Once you find the porch configuration you like, photograph it. Use it as the basis for a scale drawing.

LEFT AND BELOW: A rough drawing of your house with measurements, a photo, and some basic tools and materials are all you need to model porch options. Allow a couple of evenings for making the model. Once you build various porch elements you can mix and match to see what is most effective.

Professional design help

Unless you have some design and building background, you will need to work with professionals. Most often, this means either hiring a design-builder alone or hiring an architect as well as a design-builder.

You may find yourself in the middle of a conflicted relationship: Some builders see architects as not fully grounded in the realities of construction, and architects often think of builders as lacking in imagination and closed to unusual ideas. But this kind of tension can be creative.

Design-builders

If you already have solid ideas about your design, you may need only a design-builder. They are a varied lot. Some swing hammers along with their construction crews while others concentrate only on design, customer relations, and oversight of the job. Some take great pride in their designs while others have only a few design ideas and are more concerned with construction.

Regardless of the team you gather, bear in mind that it's rare for a construction project to proceed completely as expected. You will almost certainly encounter obstacles and issues that require changes to the plan. Good design-builders tends to make these changes quickly because they are close to the job, whereas it may take several days for an architect to get back to you with a design decision or recommendation.

When choosing a builder, look beyond the initial impression. Many a charming builder turns out to be unreliable, and many a gruff guy turns out to be a sweetheart who really cares about doing a good job. Price is also not a completely reliable predictor: The one with the

WHAT IT TAKES
Convert a deck to a porch?

Why not build a full porch on top of a deck? Reusing those piers and structural members may seem to make sense. To see if your deck can handle being transformed into a porch, measure the overall deck footprint and measure the spans and dimensions of the joists and beams as well as the size of the posts. Estimate the dimensions of the footings. Take the information to your building department or to a designer. If your deck was built very solidly and has footings in the right places, you may be allowed to build post-and-beam walls or pillars to support a roof. You may have to add some footings and posts under the deck first to strengthen it. However, don't be surprised if you have to tear out the deck and start over, since deck footings and posts are often not considered strong enough to support a porch roof. You may want to upgrade the decking anyway.

Mick Feduniec, a design-builder in North Carolina, notes that "homeowners are generally a lot smarter than they used to be, and they know what they like."

cheaper price may be the slap-it-up type, but not always; there are plenty of slap-dash builders who charge plenty, and some really competent builders with reasonable prices. Still, it's often the case that better builders and designers charge more and are worth it in the long run. The most reliable guide in selecting a builder? Take a good look at some completed porches and talk with several previous customers to get a sense of what you can expect.

If you start with solid ideas about what you want, a design-builder will be better able to meet your needs. Talk through the details—for instance, how you want the eaves and trim details to look, and the types of posts and railing components you're after. He should be willing to take your wishes seriously.

Mick Feduniec, a design-builder in North Carolina, notes that "homeowners are generally a lot smarter than they used to be, and they know what they like." And they expect good results. "Usually, this means matching everything from the house on the porch," he says. "Shingles, fascia, soffits, trim, gutters—we make sure they all match seamlessly, so the porch looks like it was always there."

Feduniec notes that it all starts with how the roofline will work out. "How it ties back into the house is the tricky part," he says. "It's rare to have a roofline with no obstacles in the way." This sometimes requires extra rooflines and angles where needed in order to make the junction between porch and house appear seamless.

Like many builders, Feduniec observes that "when an architect draws something on paper, it doesn't always work out in the field." Builders almost universally talk of how architects ask for things that simply cannot be built.

This is not necessarily a criticism of architects, simply a remodeling reality. Builders encounter problems no one anticipated—even when they drew the plans themselves.

Architects

According to architect Amy Reineri, "An architect brings vision that goes beyond typical construction." She has noticed that builders often have a stock view of how things should be built and are reluctant to do anything out of the ordinary. Often, it is not the builder but the subcontractors—especially the framers—who have a hard time thinking unconventionally. "Carpenters can be incredibly conservative," she says. The architect's role is to get builders out of a rut so they can truly meet the individual needs and desires of the client.

For instance, some contractors want to build eaves the same way they always have and are resistant to different methods. If you want exposed rather than covered rafters (or vice versa), an architect may need to argue for them. Extra-high windows, unusual railings, and electrical service beyond the ordinary are other examples of things an architect is more likely to come up with.

Engineers

Structural engineers are skilled at calculating loads and stresses, so they can compute whether a structure will remain firm and free of deflection. For example, if a porch's gable roof intersects with a gable on the house in such a way that excessive snow can accumulate, then load requirements may be increased. If you want to include a heavy fireplace or a hot tub in your porch, an engineer can

spec how to beef up the framing or how to construct a foundation to support it.

An engineer is not needed for most jobs, but one can take the place of an architect if you need to get the plans stamped. Engineers may be less expensive and easier to work with than architects. Often, you can present the plans to an engineer and get them approved in a timely manner. However, an engineer is not schooled in making porches look good, which is why architects and design-builders often work in tandem with structural engineers.

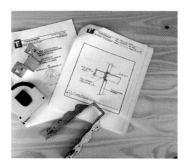

WHAT IT TAKES
Do you need a stamp?

Many building departments require that you get plans approved by a licensed architect or structural engineer. The approval takes the form of a stamp placed on the plans. The architect or engineer stamp grants a seal of approval for the porch's structural integrity, supplying expertise that may otherwise be too time-consuming or specialized for the building department to handle.

Those vital, all-important details

Once you have a plan, go over the specifics with a fine-tooth comb, and make sure to include the amenities and details that make a porch a part of a home.

The trim you want

Especially if you have an older home, it may not be possible to buy trim pieces for the porch to match. A contractor might suggest something in the same ballpark. If you want an exact match, you'll probably have to pay extra for custom-made pieces. While trim is applied late in the game, it should be planned for from the beginning. Some trim configurations call for specialized framing. In addition, trim is costly. Often, a clever layering of dimensional lumber topped off by trim has the same visual effect as expensive millwork.

Millwork shops and some lumberyards can cut trim pieces for most any profile. Bring a sample of the trim you want to match. There will likely be an initial fee for preparing the "knives" to make the trim. After that, they will probably charge by the foot. Many builders have small wood shops where they can use a table saw and a router table to do much the same thing. Some contractors are innovative enough to use technology such as computer-driven water jet saws to cut intricate trim at a low cost.

If precisely matched custom trim is not in the budget or not a high priority, the next best thing is to make your own approximation by combining stock pieces of trim. Bring a sample of the trim you

want to match to a lumberyard or home center that carries a wide selection of stock moldings. Experiment by layering various pieces on top of one another. There's a good chance you'll find a combination that will not be obviously different when viewed from a distance.

Electrical service

Codes usually do not call for a lot in the way of wiring for a porch. You may be required only to provide a receptacle (outlet) or two and a light above the door. But many people want more, including multiple fans and light fixtures, sconces and lanterns, and plenty of receptacles.

Wiring a new porch is an opportunity to include plenty of receptacles for holiday lighting. It's a good idea to have an electrician install additional circuits, so you don't overload an existing circuit when you crank up Santa and all eight reindeer. Learn how much wattage your holiday display will use, and install ample

ABOVE: Take the time to carefully review the finished plans to make sure everything you want has been addressed. Changes can and will take place as work progresses, but some will prove costly if not included in the original design.

service. (Some high-wattage displays may require as many as six new 20-amp circuits, while newer LED lighting uses far less electricity.) Also consider having one or two receptacles controlled by a switch, so you can easily turn the display off in the daytime. Or, have things wired so a switch controls one of the plugs on a receptacle.

Lingering on a neighborly front porch is usually an alternative to watching TV; however, a special ball game may be a great occasion to haul out a widescreen television. In addition, Internet access may be well worth including in your porch. Wiring for these will require CAT-5 (or CAT-6) and coaxial cable.

Consult with both your electrician and your cable or satellite provider before construction, so you can run the wiring as the porch is framed.

Screen types

A home center or hardware store carries a few types of screening, but deck and porch specialty stores and online sources have a wider variety. For the screening itself, here are some choices:

• **Standard screening has a mesh** that is 18 openings wide by 14 openings tall per square inch, which is tight enough to keep out mosquitoes and other bugs. But in an area with no-see-ums or other very tiny bugs, you may opt for a tighter mesh.

• **Screening is usually charcoal or gray** in color. A "blockout" screening made of reflective materials and a tight mesh can provide virtual shade inside while allowing you to see outside. One-way screening preserves your privacy.

• **If you pay more and buy super-strong screening**, you won't have to worry about pet damage or people bumping into it. Strong screening is available in rolls 6 and even 10 feet wide, so you can have expansive window sections.

How will the screening be installed? There are three basic options:

• **Simply stretch the screening tight** and staple it to the posts and other framing pieces, then cover the staples with trim boards. If the screening gets damaged (which happens rarely with very strong screening types), you will need to pry off the trim boards to replace it.

• **Make screen panels** to fit snugly inside the porch's framing, and attach with screws. The panels can be removed later for repair. Window companies can usually custom-build screen panels for a reasonable price.

• **Porch window units,** or storm-and-screen units, are made by a variety of manufacturers. Some have glass or acrylic panels that can be removed in the summer; the screen panels may also be removable. Others have sashes that can be slid up or removed.

ABOVE: The multiple facets of this fascia trim require framing planned for early in the design process. Trim is too expensive—and too effective a design ingredient—to be a last-minute decision.

WHAT IT TAKES
Know your setbacks and utilities

Municipalities have local setback requirements that tell you how close a porch can come to property lines. These requirements can be confusing; for instance you may need to measure from the near edge of a road, or from its centerline. Both an architect and a design-builder should be well aware of the specific setback requirements that apply to your jurisdiction.

Before digging holes, be sure the builder locates all buried utility lines, such as gas, electric, sewer, and water supply. Utility companies should come out and mark the locations using small flags or spray paint. Also be sure not to cover up utility meters attached to the house. Some may have to be moved in advance of construction.

structure

Once you've developed a general plan, it is time to think through how things will come together. Understanding **WHAT IT TAKES TO BUILD A PORCH** will give you insights on how best to complete the project. One of the most helpful insights is learning **WHAT YOU CAN DO**—and can't do—yourself. For example, if you are handy, you may want to tackle most of the construction, perhaps subbing out only the foundation. Or, you may want to handle the framing only and call in the pros for finish work. Or, perhaps you'll prefer to contract the whole job out. This chapter will help you decide which route to take. You'll also gain insight on **HOW BEST TO SPEND YOUR MONEY**. For example, if you have a low-pitch roof, you may opt for no-frills roofing material. After all, little of it will be seen from the curb. The money saved can be better used on things like custom balusters or high-end light fixtures.

Porch anatomy

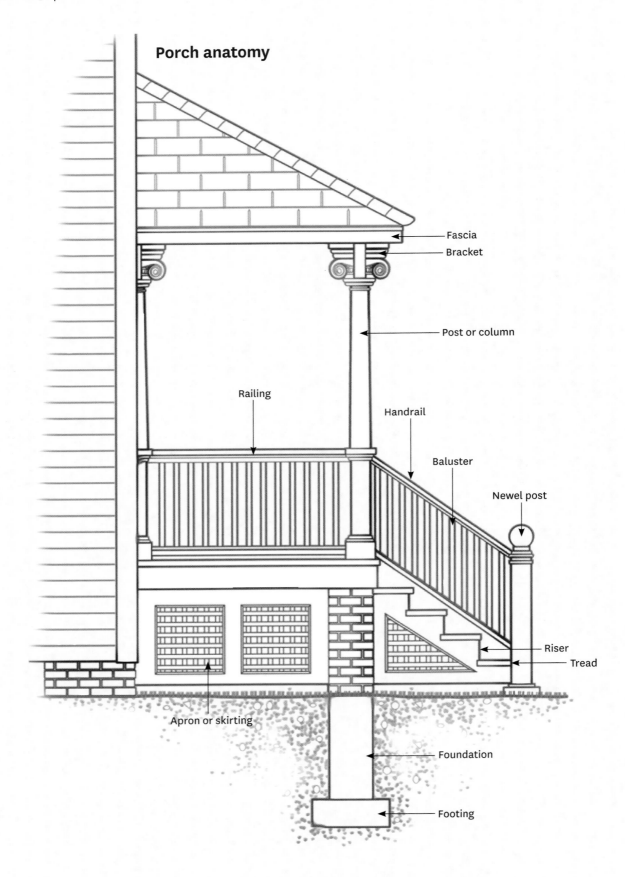

Fascia

Bracket

Post or column

Railing

Handrail

Baluster

Newel post

Riser

Tread

Apron or skirting

Foundation

Footing

Anatomy of a porch

To turn the porch of your dreams into reality, gain a thorough understanding of all the components and how they are assembled.

You'll need to decide where to access your porch from inside, settle on the appropriate type of foundation, and select materials for flooring, walls, and ceilings. Making these decisions early will help your project proceed smoothly and efficiently.

Familiarize yourself with the available options to make the wisest choices regarding style, budget, and future maintenance. Some elements, such as wood posts and railings, offer unmatched beauty and crisp details but require periodic maintenance. Polyurethane or cellular PVC elements may cost more up front but save money down the road. To maintain your budget, make firm decisions about materials before construction begins.

Porches are distinctive living spaces because they are exposed to heat, cold, sun, rain, and even snow. Select weather-resistant materials and finishes that are specifically designed to withstand season after season of the conditions your region dishes out.

A porch appears to be a less complex structure than it actually is. It has many components, each of which serves a specific purpose. It's a good idea to have a basic understanding of porch construction and terminology so you can communicate effectively with your building contractor and other professionals involved in the design and construction of your porch. The illustration *opposite* introduces the essential terms.

Footings and foundations

Any structure attached directly to your house is required to have a concrete or block foundation that complies with local building codes. The foundation must be deep enough to be unaffected by precipitation and freezing temperatures. In moderate climates the necessary depth might be only 12–18 inches, but in cold climates it must be deeper than the frost line, typically 36–48 inches below grade. Before finalizing your design or beginning construction, check with your local building authority for the specific foundation requirements in your area.

There are three types of foundations for porches. Perhaps the most common is the pier foundation, *below*, comprising poured concrete shafts spaced at regular intervals along the porch perimeter. In its simplest form, a pier supports a post that is part of the substructure of the porch. Piers sometimes are designed as columns that extend above ground to support the floor joists and beams. Simple piers stop just above grade level, and pressure-treated wood posts support the substructure. Often piers are

Pier foundation

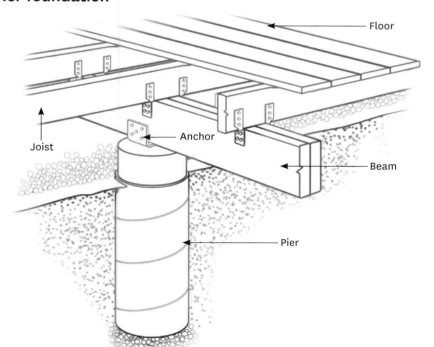

Floor

Joist

Anchor

Beam

Pier

OPPOSITE: Porch vocabulary is worth coming to terms with. That way, you can talk the talk with architects and contractors, and be clear when ordering materials from your local lumberyard or home center.

LEFT: A pier footing is one of the simplest ways to undergird a porch floor. After boring a posthole and adding a layer of gravel, a cardboard tube form is inserted to bring the pier up to the desired height. Once the form is filled with concrete, an anchor is inserted to hold a beam or post.

hidden behind a skirting of decorative lattice or other type of screening. Piers can also be formed with flat sides that are then veneered with brick or stone.

To build a porch at grade level, use a slab foundation, *right*. Slabs can be covered with a variety of top-quality finish materials, including brick, ceramic tile, or cut stone. Any framing members that come in direct contact with the slab should be pressure-treated wood.

The most substantial approach is a foundation of concrete block or formed concrete veneered with brick, stone, or stucco, *below*. This method uses more materials and is more labor-intensive, making it a more expensive option. It is sometimes used for houses that have masonry siding or a masonry foundation so that the new porch foundation blends seamlessly with existing materials. Solid foundation walls need built-in vents to promote air circulation and prevent moisture from building up underneath the porch.

Slab foundation

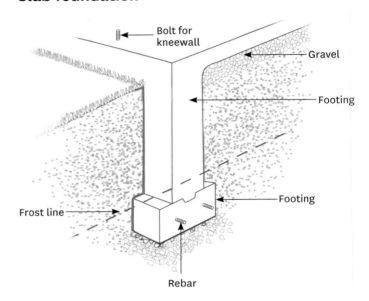

Block foundation

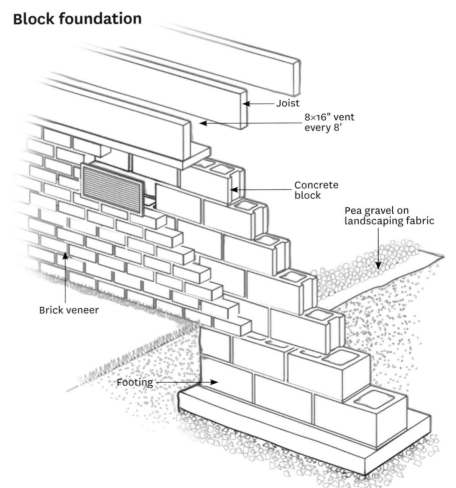

ABOVE: Foundation and floor all in one, a slab is an ideal solution for ground-level porches and the preferred surface for brick or tile flooring. In mild climates, pouring a separate footing before adding the foundation may not be required.

RIGHT: A block foundation looks great and will put your porch on a firm footing, but prepare for a serious investment. Long-term it requires minimal maintenance, without the painting and eventual replacement cost of a wood skirting. Concrete blocks bear the brunt of the support, with more expensive fired brick used mostly for looks. Don't scrimp on venting. Add vents as your region requires to avoid paint failure and rot in the porch structure.

When landscaping masks a porch's foundation, unadorned posts and piers offer support that is simple, inexpensive, and entirely adequate.

WHAT IT TAKES
Ledger logic

A poorly installed ledger has been the downfall—literally—of many a porch. It is critical that a ledger be bolted, not nailed, to wall framing members—ideally to the rim joist set on your house's foundation. Siding is removed to give the ledger stability and solid contact with the house. Flashing protects the wall from moisture incursion. Some codes require a method that holds the ledger out from the siding with beveled backer boards.

Ledger

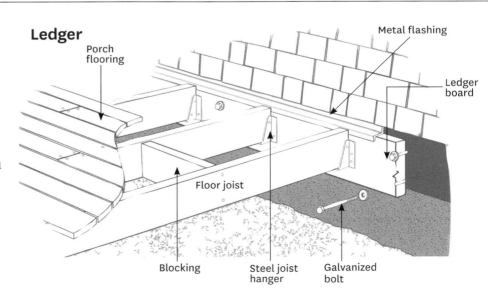

Porch flooring

Metal flashing

Ledger board

Floor joist

Blocking

Steel joist hanger

Galvanized bolt

Substructure

The substructure of a wood-frame porch is similar to a simple deck. Ledgers—the structural members attached to the house—team up with posts to support floor joists.

When joist spans get too long, beams add support. However, unlike a deck, a porch has posts that extend upward to support the roof, aided by ledgerlike members that tie the roof structure to the house. All this is accomplished using 4×4 or 6×6 posts (or manufactured columns) and 2× lumber. The type of wood used for such framing falls into one of two broad categories.

Pressure-treated (PT) lumber, usually pine or fir, is infused with chemicals that make it extremely rot-resistant. The chemicals also give the wood a green or brown cast, which can be stained or painted if needed. While PT lumber is no longer treated with arsenic compounds, always wear protective clothing, eye protection, and a dust mask when working with it. When purchasing PT lumber, look for stock that is straight, dry, and free of loose knots.

Some lumber species, such as cedar, redwood, and cypress, are resistant to rot and insects, a quality most characteristic of the heartwood, the dense center core of the tree. Exotic species such as ipe, cambara, and meranti are generally more durable, but are more difficult to work with and more expensive.

LEFT: Attractive, inexpensive, and effective, simple lattice panels offer traditional cloaking for a porch foundation.

OPPOSITE TOP: Brick gives a porch an elegant air of quiet dignity and unyielding stability.

Why follow codes?

Health, safety, and preserving your property value—that's what codes exist for and why it is in your interest to follow them. Here are some examples:

Span requirements ensure that your porch won't sag or collapse.

A porch more than two steps above ground must have a railing. Codes dictate how high the railing must be to eliminate a falling hazard.

Most codes require handrails on stairs as an aid to people less able to handle steps and to protect the unwary from falls.

Strict rules often dictate how ledgers are attached to your house and how they are flashed (see "Ledger logic," *opposite*). Dodging these can lead to a ledger that might part from the house.

Post anchors set into piers and foundations are stipulated so posts don't slip off their base. Similarly, adequate joist hangers and fasteners assure that your porch holds together in the long run.

- In cold areas, codes require that footings and foundations extend below the frost line so the porch won't heave upward as soil freezes and expands.
- Municipalities have learned that porches may later be enclosed and become year-round living space. Sound construction assures that the space with be livable.

Spans

Recommended beam spans

Distance between posts, using No. 2 and better Southern pine or Douglas fir

Beam	Joists span up to	Beam span
4×6	6′	6′
4×8	6′	8′
4×8	8′	7′
4×8	11′	6′
4×10	6′	10′
4×10	8′	9′
4×10	10′	8′
4×10	12′	7′

Recommended joist spans

Distance a joist spans between a beam and a ledger or between beams, using No. 2 and better Southern pine or Douglas fir

Joist	If joists are spaced	Span
2×6	16″	9 1/2′
2×6	24″	8′
2×8	16″	13′
2×8	24″	10 1/2′
2×10	16″	16 1/2′
2×10	24″	13 1/2′

As with a deck, a key framing member is the ledger board—the piece of lumber installed directly against the house. The ledger board usually is fastened in place with heavy galvanized bolts or lag screws. To prevent moisture and debris from getting between the ledger board and the house, the top seam should be carefully flashed with galvanized metal flashing.

For raw posts, 4×4 and 6×6 are standard. Use 2×6, 2×8, 2×10, and 2×12 lumber for joists and beams according to the span requirements of your municipal code. The table *at left* shows typical span recommendations.

Floor framing

The configuration of your frame will depend on the flooring you use. First of all, it will need to slope away from the house if you opt for tongue-and-groove, tile, or any type of flooring that is not gapped for drainage. You'll need to incline the frame away from the house by a ¼-inch drop for every foot of floor between the house and the front of the porch. For example, if your floor spans 10 feet, it should slope downward 2½ inches.

In addition, tongue-and-groove must be installed with the seams running perpendicular to the side of the house. That way,

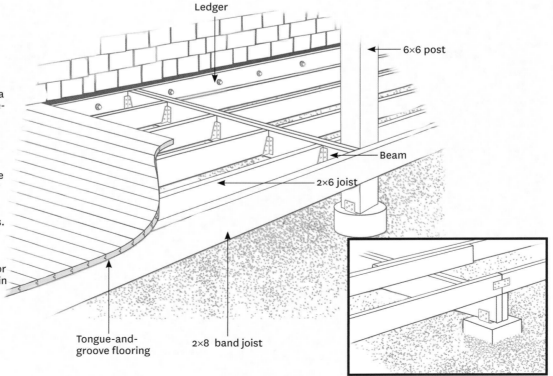

Floor frame with beam

For proper drainage, a solid floor like tongue-and-groove flooring should slope slightly away from the house, dropping about ¼ inch for every foot of run. Planks need to be placed perpendicular to the wall so water doesn't lodge in the joints between pieces. That means joists should be parallel to the house, either attached to a beam, or set atop it, as shown in the inset image.

Ledger

6×6 post

Beam

2×6 joist

Tongue-and-groove flooring

2×8 band joist

the water will drain down the length of the board, not lodge in the joint between it and adjacent planks. As a consequence, framing must be parallel to the house.

If you use decking, the standard gap between the planks is sufficient for drainage. That means you can run the flooring parallel to the house. The frame joists will run perpendicular to the house, a shorter span that shouldn't require a beam.

In times past, joists and beams could be toe-nailed to each other using other 16-penny (16d) nails. In most areas today, joist hangers and other special fasteners are required instead. These add to the cost, but simplify framing and assure long-lasting, secure joints. Deck screws have supplanted nails for most framing purposes because of their superior holding power, longevity, and—not to be underestimated—ease of being backed out when mistakes happen.

Posts and columns

Posts and columns, along with stairs and railing treatments, are the most visible features of a porch and are well worth careful planning. Posts support the roof; the railing system—sometimes called a balustrade—runs between the posts. Local building codes determine the minimum size and the spacing of the posts. Similarly, the balustrade must comply with codes. Most codes specify a distance of not greater than 4 inches between balusters—a gap too small for a child to fall through.

Check with your local building department before finalizing your design. After that, it's a matter of aesthetics. The size and spacing of posts should be in harmony with the architectural style of your house and the overall look of your porch. Likewise, the balustrade should be designed as an integral element of the overall porch design.

A post can be as simple as a 4×4, though be careful that it does not look too spindly—a common mistake in porch design. A post should look substantial and in scale with the rest of the house. Beefier options might be a plain 6×6 post or a built-up column with a structural core of a 4×4, 6×6, or several sandwiched pieces of 2×6 framing lumber.

Manufactured posts and columns include turned solid-wood or laminated types, as well as those made of materials that successfully mimic wood. Some improve on wood. For example, fiberglass and fiberglass composites are immune to rot. Equally hardy are high-density polyurethane and polyethylene posts.

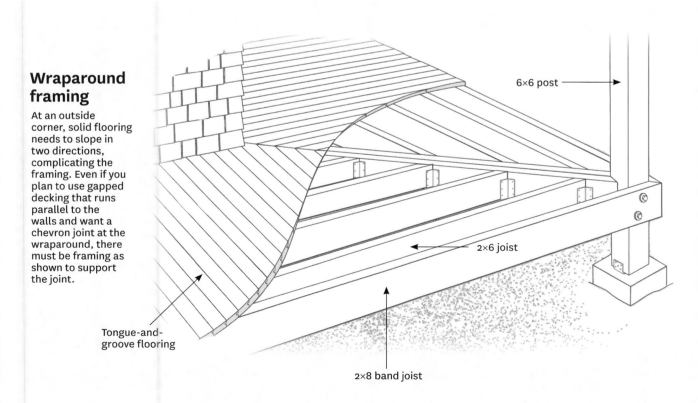

Wraparound framing

At an outside corner, solid flooring needs to slope in two directions, complicating the framing. Even if you plan to use gapped decking that runs parallel to the walls and want a chevron joint at the wraparound, there must be framing as shown to support the joint.

Tongue-and-groove flooring

6×6 post

2×6 joist

2×8 band joist

These have galvanized steel pipe or laminated hardwood as a core, fleshed out with high-density foam. Both are woodlike in feel and workability. They sound like wood when you knock on them and take fasteners just like wood, making rails, brackets, and decorative items easy to attach. Vinyl columns are less expensive, but are disconcertingly hollow. Often, builders choose to initially support the roof with rough posts that can be replaced with finished columns toward the end of the job when risk of any damage is past.

Some architectural styles call for a masonry base combined with a column, *below*. Although this complex approach will boost your budget, the architectural panache it brings can be well worth the investment. True brick or stone masonry requires a substantial footing, but by use of a laminated through-post and some clever case work, the same effect can be achieved, as shown in the illustration *at right*.

Column with masonry base

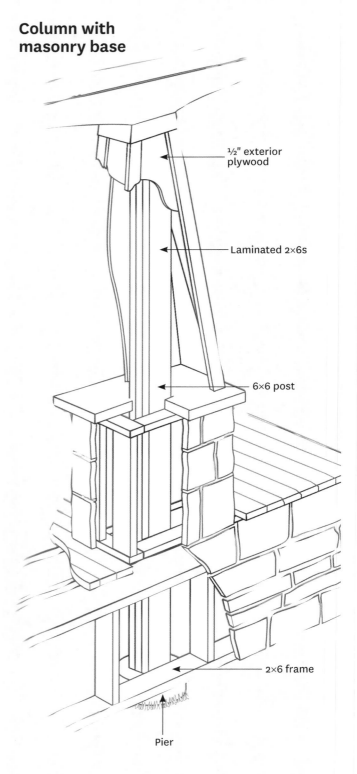

- ½" exterior plywood
- Laminated 2×6s
- 6×6 post
- 2×6 frame
- Pier

Real masonry bases with tapered wooden columns are a classic Craftsman-style feature.

Post on a pier

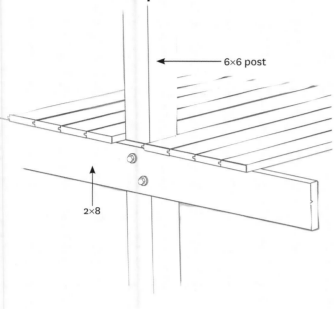

6×6 post

2×8

A post that rests directly on a pier, runs through the floor, and supports the run is one of the simplest and soundest post approaches.

Built-up post

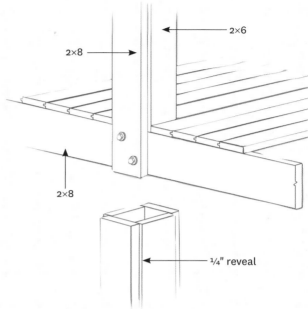

2×6

2×8

2×8

¼" reveal

A built-up post made with 2×6s and 2×8s attaches firmly to framing and adds visual interest. Adding 1× lumber to a 4×4 or 6×6 post can achieve a similar effect.

WHAT IT TAKES
Manufactured posts

Here's the typical scenario for installing a manufactured post. Begin by ordering your column based on your plan measurements. Construct the roof using temporary posts made of doubled 2×4s. When it is time to install the column, measure the height and subtract the thickness of the base and capital. Trim the column as needed at its top and bottom. Paint the cut ends according to the manufacturer's instructions, and apply the moisture barrier membrane provided.

Using a plumb bob, mark the locations of the base and capital. Use a metal jack post to support the roof. Extend the post an extra ¼ inch to allow for inserting the new post. Remove the temporary support. Slide the column into place and check for plumb. Carefully remove the temporary support, and fasten the base and capital according to the manufacturer's instructions.

Roof

Like the floor framing, roof framing is supported by posts and a ledgerlike member attached to the house.

Rafters are typically made of 2×6s for full-size porches, 2×4s for porticos and small overhangs. The roof should harmonize with the existing architectural style of the house—a consideration that bears upon the framing. For example, if your home has deep fascia, the framing will have to be planned to accommodate something similar on your porch.

In addition, you'll need to think ahead to the type of ceiling treatment you want—it will affect how you frame and sheath your porch roof. You may prefer to enclose the framing members or leave them visible from underneath. Enclosed framing has two versions: vaulted ceilings include finish materials that cover the roof rafters; drop ceilings feature ceiling joists installed horizontally, to which ceiling material is attached. Enclosed ceilings have an advantage over open ceilings because electrical wiring and cables can be easily installed in them and will be concealed behind the ceiling material. This greatly simplifies installing lighting fixtures and ceiling fans.

If you prefer to expose the framing from below, take special care in selecting the rafter material so it is free of gouges and loose knots. You may want to invest in extra hefty rafters of "No. 1" or "Select" lumber. Make sure the sheathing is thick enough to hide the tips of nails securing the roofing material. Use ¾-inch-thick sheathing (½-inch is standard) and roofing nails no longer than ¾ inch to ensure that nails don't punch through. Beaded board, tongue-and-groove planks, or a good grade of plywood make an attractive surface. However you construct the roof, be sure the seam between the house siding and the porch roof is sealed against leaks with flashing—a strip of galvanized sheet metal typically bent in an L shape (see *illustration below*). One leg of the flashing installs under existing siding, and the other extends over the top of the new porch roofing. Don't skimp on this stage. Poor flashing leads to a leaky roof and expensive damage to the wall.

Prep for roofing

Whatever types of roofing you choose, you'll need to apply roofing felt, drip edge, and perhaps ice-dam material. Roofing felt provides a vapor barrier to protect the plywood or OSB (oriented strand board) sheathing from moisture damage.

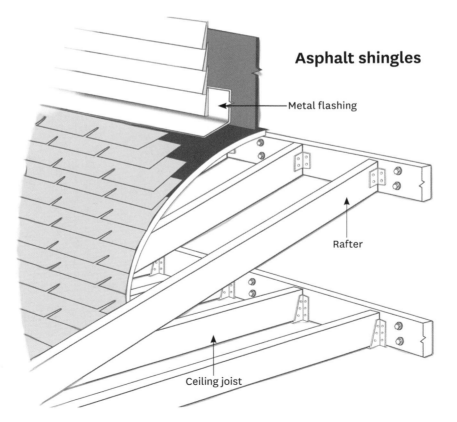

Asphalt shingles

Metal flashing

Rafter

Ceiling joist

This roof with its enclosed ceiling uses 2×6s for rafters and ceiling joists. Both are attached to the house with ledgerlike framing members. These should be bolted—not nailed— to wall framing members. Sheathing of ½- to ¾-inch plywood or OSB (oriented strand board) is nailed to the rafters, followed by roofing felt and then shingles or other roofing materials. Walls should be carefully flashed to avoid moisture damage. If the slope of your roof intersects a wall, use step flashing pieces that slip under each shingle and behind the siding.

At the lower part of the roof near the eaves, a self-adhesive membrane applied instead of felt provides added protection against ice incursion.

Drip edge flashing applied along the edges of the roof keeps water from seeping under the roofing. If you have a valley, prep it with a run of ice-dam material and metal valley flashing. If you enclose the ceiling, add vents to clear the roof cavity of moisture. A chimney needs special flashing and, if on a substantial slope, a tiny rooflike structure called a cricket.

Roofing

A porch can have any type of roofing as long as it has enough slope. Slope is the angle of the roof plane, typically described as a ratio of its rise in inches compared to a 12-inch run. The ratio 4:12 describes a roof that rises 4 inches in every 12 inches of run. It is sometimes expressed as "4-in-12." Shingles should not be used on flat or semi-flat (2:12 slope or less) roofs—moisture will quickly seep under the shingles and damage the porch. For similar reasons, cedar shakes should not be used on a roof with less than a 4:12 slope.

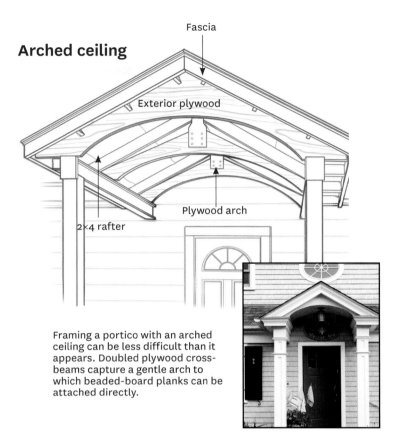

Arched ceiling

Fascia

Exterior plywood

Plywood arch

2×4 rafter

Framing a portico with an arched ceiling can be less difficult than it appears. Doubled plywood crossbeams capture a gentle arch to which beaded-board planks can be attached directly.

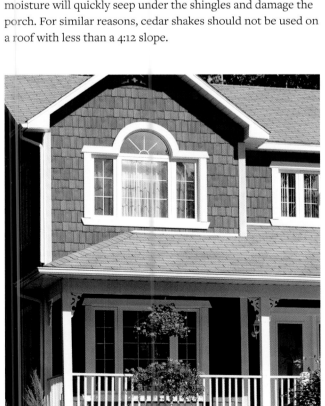

Composition shingles, made of asphalt or fiberglass, are inexpensive and easy to install. Fiberglass shingles are lighter and less prone to curling. Do not use tab shingles on a slope of 2 inches or less per foot.

Architectural shingles, also called laminated or dimensional shingles, are made by laminating a notched top layer to a solid bottom layer. They are more expensive but longer lasting than standard shingles.

Modified bitumen and EPDM (rubber) roofing have surpassed roll roofing as the most common choice for flat roofs. They come in large sheets and are extremely strong and flexible.

Roll roofing is made of the same material as asphalt or fiberglass shingles but comes in 36-inch-wide rolls. Standard roll roofing has a short life expectancy, but thicker self-adhesive types are well-suited to nearly flat roofs.

Wood shakes and shingles are made from cedar. Shakes are split; shingles are sawn. No. 1 grade shingles are made from heartwood and resist rot well. Cedar shakes and shingles can withstand prolonged exposure to sun and weather.

Vertical metal roofing, once associated with commercial applications, is now available in attractive colors ideal for residential use. Thicker grade panels last longer; check the warranty.

Slate shingles are long lasting and resistant to fire, but are expensive and need professional installation. Artificial slate shingles made of plastic or rubber are less expensive and easier to install. From the ground they look very much like slate.

Made of Portland cement and sand, concrete tiles are less expensive and easier to install than genuine clay. Like clay, they are heavy and may require special framing.

Clay tiles may be fairly flat, ribbed, or scalloped, as shown. A genuine Spanish-style clay tile roof will last indefinitely. Clay tile must be installed by a professional and will require extra framing.

Metal tile-look roofing is a light alternative to the real thing. However, it can be noisy during a heavy rainstorm.

Flooring

A porch floor should be durable, be resistant to moisture, and complement the style of your home.

It should not warp, splinter, or chip, and it should provide a smooth, safe walking surface free of defects. Despite these requirements, the options for porch floors are actually broader than those for indoor rooms. Natural stone and wood, composite flooring and decking, concrete, brick, and ceramic tiles are all suitable for an open porch partially exposed to the elements.

The type of porch foundation generally influences flooring choices. Wood floors typically are used with post-and-pier foundations that have a substructure of beams and joists. Ceramic tile, cut stone, and brick usually are reserved for slab foundations. Tile and stone, however, can be used on elevated porches, providing the substructure is designed to withstand the considerable weight, the subfloor has absolutely no give to it (cracked mortar or grout degrades quickly), and the floor is pitched to shed water. Indoor-outdoor carpets may be installed over either wood or concrete slabs.

Wood floors

Years ago, porch floors traditionally were made using tongue-and-groove fir flooring. Fir is strong and durable, and doesn't readily warp or cup. Today, however, top-quality fir boards that are free from defects such as knots are increasingly rare and expensive. The tongue-and-groove boards that might serve as flooring are from softer wood species, such as pine or hemlock, and are much more prone to warping and cupping when exposed to the elements. This type of lumber also is susceptible to rot caused by moisture trapped inside the tongue-and-groove joints. For these reasons, most builders prefer not to use tongue-and-groove boards for porch flooring. A better choice is square-edge lumber that has been treated with a wood preservative or sealer prior to installation. Over time, the joints between the boards will open slightly, allowing rainwater or melted snow to drain.

ABOVE: Composite tongue-and-groove flooring made from hardwood fiber and polypropylene, polyethylene, or PVC is supplanting painted fir. It is almost indistinguishable from fir flooring and much easier to maintain.

LEFT: Brick tiles are cool, good-looking, and impervious to moisture. Sealing them regularly keeps them stain resistant and easy to clean. A concrete base is ideal.

Wood decking wears well and has a handsome, informal look. Hidden deck fasteners are a great idea for a porch where the unsightliness of screwheads or nailheads would detract from the beauty of the floor.

All sides of each board should be coated with a preservative that is allowed to dry for two or three days before being installed. Sealer should be applied to any freshly cut ends before they are fastened to joists.

Another option is to use pressure-treated wood. This chemically treated, rot-resistant material is often shipped from the factory while still moist. Bundles should be separated and the boards allowed to dry completely before installing. The color of pressure-treated wood is dull green or brown. If you want to paint pressure-treated lumber, buy kiln-dried lumber, or wait about six months for the wood to dry completely before painting.

While a natural wood finish makes for an attractive floor, a painted floor adds color and some protection against the elements. Top-quality exterior paints made specifically for floors offer an especially tough finish that resists scrapes and scratches. For added durability, allow the paint to dry thoroughly, then apply two coats of exterior-grade, clear polyurethane.

Composite flooring

Made of wood fibers and plastic resins, many of which are recycled materials, wood composites are the surface of choice for most new decks and equally desirable for porches. Tongue-and-groove composite flooring uses no visible fasteners and is visually indistinguishable from painted wood flooring. In fact, it looks so much like the real thing that it has been used in historical restorations. It comes in a limited range of colors, but can be painted. Floor joists must be no more than 16 inches apart—8 inches if you choose to place the flooring diagonally. Standard composite decking is also a good-looking, hard-wearing choice, especially for an exposed porch floor that gets a lot of rain. The gaps between the decking drain water quickly.

Masonry floors

Tile, stone, and brick make excellent flooring for porches. These materials are water-resistant and are classic finishes for high-moisture areas. They install readily over a concrete slab. New tile materials and installation techniques allow tile to be used successfully even in cold climates where freeze-thaw cycles once made it difficult to keep tile in good repair on an unheated porch.

Tile and stone can be installed on elevated porches, although the additional structural materials required to support the considerable weight makes porch installation costly and rare. Refer to local building codes to determine the requirements for the substructure. For stability and to prevent cracking mortar and grout lines, a subfloor not less than 1¼ inches thick usually is required. The thickness generally is created by using sheets of ¾-inch, exterior-grade plywood covered by ½-inch-thick sheets of cement backerboard—a material designed specifically for tile installations. As with any porch floor, creating a slope so that water runs away from the house is imperative.

TOP: Hardwood or composite deck tiles make handsome porch floors that drain readily (plastic feet hold them slightly above the subfloor). They install without fasteners and require only minimal cutting.

ABOVE: Cut slate is durable and beautiful, providing an elegant, no-fuss porch surface. It is light enough to be applied to a wood subfloor as long as it is stable with absolutely no give to it. Be cautious of metal outdoor furniture—slate can scratch.

With its capacity to be tinted, formed, and stamped, concrete offers versatility for a porch floor. It is cool and easy to maintain and, should you want to add a tile or stone surface later, an excellent substrate.

Indoor-outdoor carpet and rugs

Indoor-outdoor carpet is designed to withstand moisture and temperature fluctuations, and it is treated to resist the fading effects of ultraviolet light associated with exposure to direct sunlight. The notorious grass-green variety often adhered to slabs is not the only color you have to choose from. Outdoor carpet is available in a wide variety of patterns, colors, and textures. Indoor-outdoor carpet is another flooring option that allows you to create a comfortable living area in a porch environment.

The carpet is adhered to the subfloor using a strong, water-resistant glue. Solvent-base glue generally is superior to latex-base glue because it can be applied in a wider range of weather conditions and is more water-resistant. It installs readily over concrete slabs that are dry and free from alkali residue. For porches with wood substructures, indoor-outdoor carpet requires a smooth subfloor. It can be installed over regular board flooring, but a subfloor of exterior-grade plywood is better. A stable plywood subfloor will help the carpet maintain its good looks for years. Waxed or oiled wood floors require resurfacing before they can be used as a subfloor for glued-down indoor-outdoor carpet. If you decide to install indoor-outdoor carpet, consider it a permanent commitment—removing it is difficult.

If your tastes change too frequently to commit to the permanence of indoor-outdoor carpet, try an area rug. Area rugs provide the opportunity to update the look of your porch easily and for relatively little expense. Sisal-look synthetic rugs can cover all or most of a porch. A painted canvas floor cloth is another option that can be a lively conversation piece as well as a suitable floor covering for a porch.

Walls

Porches purposely have few walls. Any existing walls or new walls should receive careful consideration to ensure that they are integral to the overall design of the project.

Your porch will include at least one of the following three types of walls: existing exterior walls, walls made with screening material for screen porches, and low knee walls that run around the perimeter of the porch.

Existing walls

Generally, clapboard, brick, or stucco makes an attractive, durable finish and emphasizes the fact that a porch is an exterior room. Because it is already installed, it's a cost-effective wall covering. There is no need to replace siding during a porch-building project unless it is in extremely poor condition, or if replacing it is part of a larger renovation project. However, you'll want to make sure it is in good repair by replacing broken or warped wood, repainting worn surfaces, and caring for masonry by replacing missing mortar and patching cracked stucco. Once repaired, the walls will be protected from sun and precipitation by the porch roof and should remain in good condition for many years.

If you don't care for the appearance of your siding, camouflage it with porch furnishings, such as shelves, and tall potted plants. Arrange seating so that it faces away from the porch walls. Add interesting details to porch posts and balustrades that draw attention away from the walls. A stylish front door or a new window gives plain walls a dash of character.

RIGHT: Like picture frames, small windows add interest and restore interior light hampered by the porch roof.

OPPOSITE TOP: A potting area at one end of a porch is both functional and decorative.

OPPOSITE BOTTOM: Wall brackets are indoor-outdoor accessories that suit a porch well.

Upgrade your walls

If the current siding on your home reflects poorly on your new porch, but replacing it is not within the budget, try these fix-up ideas:

Brick. Remove efflorescence—a white powdery substance—with water and a stiff brush. Or, paint the brick.

Stucco. Repair cracks by filling them with acrylic silicone caulk. Caulk is available in several colors. Try to match the color of the existing stucco. Touch up the repaired area with paint.

Vinyl or metal. Fill small holes with caulk that closely matches the color of the original siding. Use touch-up paint to disguise small scratches.

Board. Replace badly damaged or split boards to prevent water from leaking behind the boards and doing major damage to your home. Prime and paint.

Any type. Disguise less-than-perfect existing walls by adding accessories to your porch. Some suggestions:
- Place a decorative shelf enhanced with lush plants along the existing wall.
- Hang inexpensive art that won't be damaged by humidity and moisture.
- Set up a floor screen of wood, metal, garden latticework, or bifold doors in front of a particularly offensive section of siding.
- Install window boxes under windows along the porch wall. Plant with colorful flowers.
- Display casual collectibles such as pottery, baskets, or shells on a baker's rack or on decorative shelves.

Window screening options

Developed in the 1800s to keep pests out of houses, fine-mesh insect screening is essentially unchanged from its original design. Manufactured in several widths, it can be used for seamless panels up to 60 inches wide. Consider large openings carefully—the wider it is, the more susceptible the screen is to sagging.

Openings 42 inches wide or less are recommended. Remember that small children and pets can wreck the lower portion of screened walls, and large openings increase the cost of repairs. One solution is to build low knee walls 24 to 32 inches high between the vertical structural members.

You can attach screen material directly to framing members, but a better method is to create removable screen panels. Panels should fit precisely between framing members and are held in place with clips. This way, they remove easily for repair or storage. Include storage space for screens as part of your plan—a great use for the space beneath the porch.

Screen typically is made of fiberglass mesh, aluminum wire mesh, or copper mesh. The chart *at right* lists the pros and cons of these materials. Any of the materials will keep insects from invading your porch. Beyond that, selection is a matter of weighing benefits and costs. If you choose a fiberglass or aluminum wire screen, the selection of color is a matter of visual preference—dark finishes resist glare and are good choices for sunny locations.

Screening choices

MATERIALS

FIBERGLASS MESH

Pros
- Lightweight
- Easy to work with
- Won't discolor over time
- Available in several colors: gray, black, charcoal

Cons
- Tends to stretch
- Won't recover original tautness if stretched
- Tears easily

ALUMINUM MESH

Pros
- Resists corrosion
- Tougher than fiberglass
- Resists stretching
- Resists tearing
- Available in several colors: gray, black, charcoal

Cons
- Discolors over time

COPPER SCREEN

Pros
- Tougher than fiberglass and aluminum
- Holds its shape
- Coppery color that ages to a mellow brown

Cons
- Expensive
- No color options

ABOVE: A simple screened porch offers all the pleasures of the outdoors, with less sun and fewer bugs.

OPPOSITE: Relax in the shade, listening to birds or enjoying a good book. A screened porch is an elegantly casual refuge.

RIGHT: A knee wall, heavy ornamentation, and a prominent gabled roof make the porch a vital component of this Victorian home.

BELOW: Shutters create the illusion of a knee wall that can quickly disappear.

OPPOSITE: A knee wall helps define the sweeping curve of a shingle-clad porch.

Knee walls

Some styles of houses include low walls, sometimes called knee walls, as part of the porch design. Shingle-style houses and Craftsman bungalows are two architectural types that frequently have solid knee walls running along the porch perimeter, with support columns for the roof placed on the load-bearing portions of the walls.

Most building codes require porches with floors more than 30 inches above the ground to be protected by railings that are at least 36 inches high and have balusters spaced no more than 4 inches apart—requirements satisfied by the construction of a knee wall. However, solid knee walls add considerable mass to the exterior of a home and should be carefully designed to fit its style. Usually this seamless appearance is accomplished by covering the knee wall with the same exterior siding material used on the rest of the house.

To allow moisture to drain from porch flooring, solid walls should include holes or scuppers at floor level. Typically, scuppers are 2 or 3 inches high, 6 to 8 inches wide, and are spaced every 6 to 8 feet around the knee wall.

The allure of lattice

An elevated porch inevitably has open space beneath it that needs to be screened from critters, blowing refuse, and errant soccer balls. There are several ways to hide the space, but lattice has long been the material of choice. Wood lattice panels, often made of marginal pressure-treated battens, have all but been supplanted by vinyl alternatives. Vinyl is stronger and, best of all, doesn't require tedious painting. Vinyl is available in panels with stars, palms, and other elaborate cutouts to choose from.

If lattice is not your cup of tea, open-work brick, vertical slats, or solid skirting with fanciful cutouts can serve the same purpose. Tip: Add an access door for storing unwieldy and seldom used items like screens and extension ladders.

Ceilings

A porch ceiling can be one of three types: open, vaulted, or drop. Each has its own unique considerations.

An open ceiling reveals the rafters supporting the porch roof. A vaulted ceiling follows the roof pitch with finish materials attached directly to the rafters. A drop ceiling has finish materials applied to the undersides of horizontal ceiling joists.

Each requires a slightly different framing approach. An open ceiling uses better-than-average framing material free of the wear and tear typical of most framing lumber. Beefy laminated beams are a good choice. An open ceiling also requires forethought about the finished look because ceiling material must be applied over, not under, the rafters.

A vaulted ceiling frames up in a conventional homebuilding manner with typical framing lumber because the finish material will cover the rafters.

A drop ceiling requires ceiling joists much like the interior rooms of your house. In many ways this is the simplest type of ceiling to construct. Joists made of 2×6s are typical, though for short spans 2×4s can be used.

Because porch ceilings are well protected from the elements, many types of finish materials can be installed. Plywood or vinyl panels are the quickest. (Adding trim in a 2-foot by 2-foot grid is a stylish way to hide the seams.) Tongue-and-groove planks are a classic approach. New PVC and composite panels and planks are well suited for porches, though some benefit from a layer of plywood sheathing attached to rafters or joints for extra nailing space. Use stainless-steel or galvanized fasteners and exterior-grade paints to combat the effects of high humidity and temperature fluctuations. With some materials, space must be left for expansion—a manufacturer's requirement worth heeding to avoid unsightly warps and sags.

The classic porch ceiling material—beaded board—is a popular choice. You can create this look with individual boards, plywood sheets, or panels of PVC or aluminum.

This open ceiling shows the power of exposed rafters coupled with contrasting planks. Beefier rafters allow wider spacing than the 16 inches typical for rafters.

A vaulted ceiling provides a sense of spaciousness and gives warm air a place to go. It also looks great. The unpainted beaded board in this porch is a woodsy complement to a tree-filled view.

The clear-finished beaded-board planks on this drop ceiling reflect a warm light into the porch. The natural grain of wood and the stone column bases complement the clean colors of the wall and trim.

This vaulted ceiling includes eye-catching horizontal beams. While not always structurally necessary, they help break up a large porch into visually appealing "rooms."

Stairs and railings

Of all the elements of a porch, the stairs and railings make the clearest style statement and add the most to your home's curb appeal.

Think about it. For someone driving up to your house, the porch roof and ceiling are almost entirely hidden from view. The floor is virtually invisible until that visitor walks onto the porch. But the stairs and railings are front and center. That's a good reason to think carefully about their style and proportions, and the materials they're made of.

One challenging element of designing good-looking railings and stairs is creating even spacing between porch posts. The design must take into account the placement of stairs with regard to the main entry door, the number of supporting posts required to hold up the porch roof, and the overall length of the porch deck. Juggling these numbers and ending up with a pleasing design is no simple task. One solution is to adjust the overall size of the porch to facilitate even spacings. Another option is to adjust the placement of one or more posts to produce differences in spacings that are virtually undetectable.

RIGHT: Stone has a timeless, natural quality that adds a touch of pedigree to even a brand-new porch.

WHAT IT TAKES
Rise and run

Stairs that are easy on the stride don't happen by accident; they need to be planned carefully. For the uninitiated, this can be a real mind bender. Here's the secret to success. For ease of stepping, the deeper a stair's tread, the shorter its rise. Twice the riser height plus the run (the distance between risers) should equal between 24 and 27 inches. For example, if risers are 7 inches and runs are 11 inches, the formula works out like this: 2×7=14 (the riser height times 2) plus 11 (the tread run) equals 25, nicely within the 24 to 27 range. Very important: At either end of the stringer you need to take into account the thickness of the flooring (at the porch) and the thickness of the tread (at the landing).

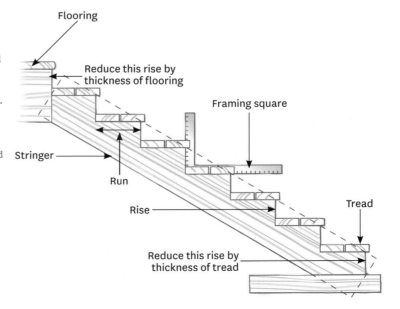

Flooring

Reduce this rise by thickness of flooring

Framing square

Stringer

Run

Rise

Tread

Reduce this rise by thickness of tread

The rugged good looks of brick make it a popular choice for steps. While brick offers built-in traction and almost no maintenance, it does require its own concrete foundation.

Simple stairs

This simple approach would be ideal for a second set of stairs on a wraparound porch or the main set of stairs on a small porch, in which case you may want to add kick plates to each step. Using metal tread brackets to support treads saves cutting two stringers—always a time-consuming job. In addition, by using unnotched stringers on either side of the stairs, you'll have more surface area to attach posts to. Complete the landing before building the stairs. Always use pressure-treated lumber for stair framing.

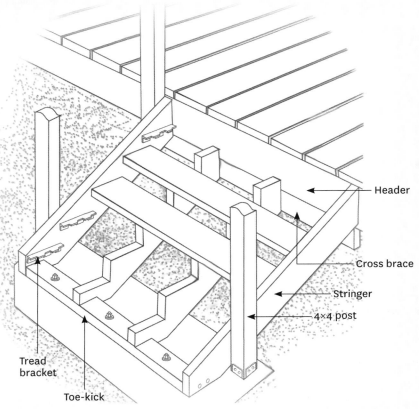

Header

Cross brace

Stringer

4×4 post

Tread bracket

Toe-kick

Deep treads

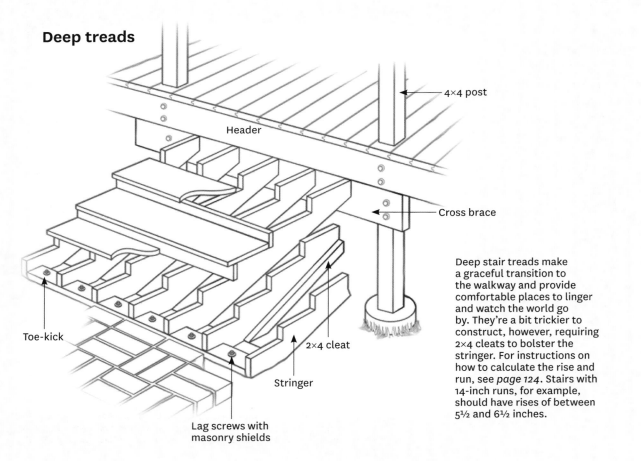

4×4 post

Header

Cross brace

Toe-kick

2×4 cleat

Stringer

Lag screws with masonry shields

Deep stair treads make a graceful transition to the walkway and provide comfortable places to linger and watch the world go by. They're a bit trickier to construct, however, requiring 2×4 cleats to bolster the stringer. For instructions on how to calculate the rise and run, see *page 124*. Stairs with 14-inch runs, for example, should have rises of between 5½ and 6½ inches.

Stairs

Whether your stairs are wood, brick, stone, or concrete, you'll need to make some basic decisions about their size. Stairs typically center on the main entryway and should be at least as wide as the doorway, including any sidelights or adjacent windows. Plan them carefully so they are easy on the stride. Check your local codes for requirements—a comfortable combination of rise and run (see "Rise and run" *page 124*) is an important safety consideration. Get it wrong and you might face an expensive rebuild.

Classic porch style aligns the front stairs with the main doorway. This approach makes the main entry clear to visitors. It also is the most efficient use of porch space, creating the shortest possible route from stairway to entry door and reserving the remainder of the porch area as living space. Include the landing at the bottom of the stairs in your plans. This area should be integral to the overall design of the stairway. A patio or walkway made of brick, concrete, or stone forms the ideal approach to stairs. Stairs have to withstand plenty of use, so choose lumber that is straight and free of knots and other defects. Pay extra for "Select" or "No. 1" grades. Some lumber sources sell 2x12s specifically approved for use as treads or stringers.

Railings

Railings are an important safety feature of stairways, raised decks, platforms, and porches. Typically, the design of the railing system is mirrored in the balustrade of the stairway. A railing system includes handrails, balusters, and posts. These parts can be made of wood, high-density urethane and molded polymers, wood covered with vinyl, cable, glass, and powder-coated aluminum.

Wood offers strength and well-defined details. Although wooden porch parts typically are made from rot-resistant redwood or cedar, they require periodic maintenance with top-quality exterior-grade paint or stain. You'll find a large variety of options from companies that specialize in wooden parts. The range of woods suitable for railings includes cedar, redwood, cypress, poplar, oak, and western hemlock.

Wooden parts covered with vinyl are the least expensive and are generally available at home improvement centers. The core is made with pressure-treated wood that provides strength and resistance to rot, and the vinyl coverings are maintenance-free. They come in standard sizes and may have to be adjusted on-site to fit individual porches.

Some home centers also offer powder-coated aluminum rail systems including posts, rails, and balusters. Such railings are very strong, require no maintenance, and install quickly. They are made to adapt to most any situation, an attribute that comes at the expense of style options.

Composite railing systems have long been used on decks but are adaptable to porches as well. They come in many colors and are simple to assemble. However, the style options are limited.

When it comes to gingerbread and trim, cypress (shown) is a tough but workable wood. Cellular PVC is another good option for gingerbread because delicate cutouts are less prone to crack upon impact. It is also easier to clean and does not have to be painted.

Railing parts made from high-density urethane, polyethylene, and PVC are virtually weather- and rot-proof and require little maintenance. Of all the types, these offer the greatest variety of sizes and styles. It's well worth visiting several online sites to view the surprising range of options.

These railings usually come from the factory with a baked-on white primer that can stand as the finish coat or be painted. PVC can be painted with 100 percent acrylic paint; polyurethane and polyethylene can be painted with any high-quality latex paint, though manufacturers do not recommend extremely dark colors. These materials are structurally sound and meet or exceed building code requirements. The parts are made as systems that fit together with little measuring or cutting.

Pioneered on decks, composite railings easily adapt to porches. Although composite components are available in a wider range of colors than other systems, the style options are limited.

Should you need custom elements such as post brackets, consider ¾-inch PVC panels. They cut easily, shape like wood, and are rot-resistant. Laminated together, they can make substantial elements that would be difficult to fabricate out of wood.

Classic railing style

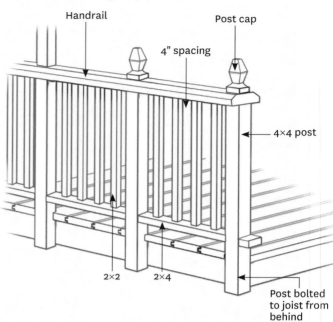

This simple approach suits most any architectural style, especially by changing the post cap profile. Narrowly spaced posts strengthen the structure and help create a more interesting design.

Stairs and railings

Building codes strictly regulate the design of stairs and railings. Although codes vary from region to region, most include these basic requirements:

Stairs. Those more than 30 inches high must have guardrails at least 34 inches high, measured from the nosing of the stairs.

Railings. These must have intermediate rails or posts or other ornamental fill that will not pass an object 4 inches in diameter (a 4-inch ball).

Stair handrails. The height of stair handrails must be between 30 and 38 inches, measured directly above the nosing of the tread. The handrail must be installed on at least one side of a stairway that has more than two risers.

Risers. The maximum height is 7¾ inches. A riser 6 inches high and a tread 12 inches deep are recommended for outdoor stairways. (Note: The dimensions of treads and risers cannot vary by more than ⅜ inch from step to step.)

Contemporary Craftsman

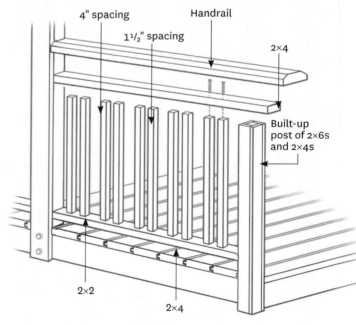

Combining built-up posts made of 2×6s and 2×4s, this approach changes things up a bit by pairing the balusters. They are fastened through the 2×4s that sandwich them, a neat way to keep the screws out of sight.

Low-profile effect

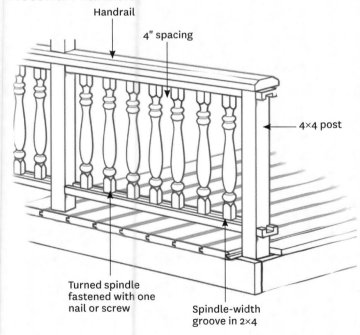

Handrail

4" spacing

2×4 top rail
behind 1×4

4×4 post

2×4 bottom
rail behind 1×4

1×4

While 2x4 top and bottom rails provide most of the strength for this design, 1×4s covering the rails add visual heft and reduce the perception of height. For a slightly more contemporary look, 2x6s could be substituted for milled handrail.

Notched posts

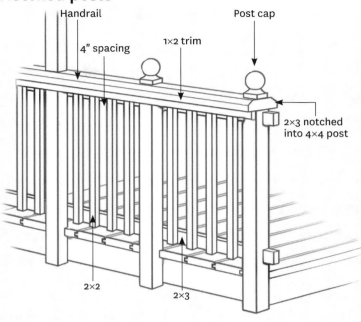

Handrail

4" spacing

1×2 trim

Post cap

2×3 notched
into 4×4 post

2×2

2×3

Notching the posts makes for a neat, solid assembly but requires a table saw and some experience making precision cuts. The notch also weakens the post somewhat, a good reason to position posts no more than 4 feet apart.

Victorian variation

Handrail

4" spacing

4×4 post

Turned spindle
fastened with one
nail or screw

Spindle-width
groove in 2×4

Turned spindles suit a wide range of traditional styles. Placing posts behind the rim joist is in keeping with older porch styles but requires notching the flooring. Complex railings like this can be assembled in sections before being attached to the posts with finishing screws driven at an angle. The top and bottom rails can be purchased with the groove already milled.

Ranch railing

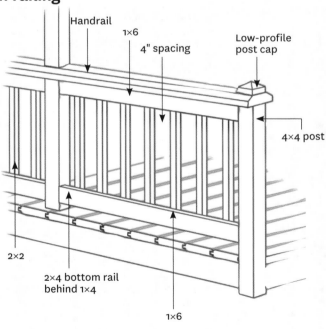

Handrail

1×6

4" spacing

Low-profile
post cap

4×4 post

2×2

2×4 bottom rail
behind 1×4

1×6

This simple and solid configuration suits a wide variety of architectural styles. A 2×6 handrail could be substituted for the milled rail. The low-profile cap gives the illusion of the post passing through the handrail.

Ramp basics

Accommodating people with special needs requires sensitive—and imaginative—solutions. This is especially true of wheelchair ramps, which may have considerable length. The architect who designed the ramp shown below had an additional consideration: His final design had to meet the approval of the local historical commission. The answer is a broad porch that houses a wheelchair ramp. Because the ramp flows side to side, the depth of the porch is in keeping with the architectural style of the house. Across the front, level railings and a curb wall present the illusion of a typical elevated porch.

Although looks may be important, the practical concerns of creating an accessible, easy-to-use ramp are primary considerations. The basic principles of ramp design specify a slope of 1 vertical inch for every 12 inches of run for unassisted (hand-operated) wheelchair use. A doorway located 30 inches above grade would require a wheelchair ramp 30 feet long for unassisted use. If the ramp is to be used exclusively by persons with assisted (motorized) wheelchairs, a slope of 2 vertical inches for every 12 inches of run is allowed. Landings in front of doors should be at least 36 inches wide and 60 inches deep for in-swinging doors, and 60 inches square for out-swinging doors.

ABOVE: Appropriate railings and surface materials make this ramp a natural extension of the home's architectural style.

RIGHT: This porch-enclosed ramp shows how a ramp can stylishly be adapted to a more traditional home without detracting from its style. Not only did it have to meet standards for accessibility, it had to pass muster with the local historical commission.

Ramps don't have to be purely utilitarian. This deck ramp would easily adapt to a low-slung porch and could be constructed with materials readily available from any home center or lumberyard.

Pergolas

Wouldn't it be great if your porch roof could magically transform itself as the seasons change, creating shade in the summer and letting in sunlight during the winter?

A pergola performs just that sort of magic. If aligned carefully, it can shelter from the heat of summer when the sun is high and allow in warming rays when the winter sun is low.

A pergola is a handy addition to a porch not only because of its all-season flexibility, but also because it can extend the transformative effect of a porch at a much lower cost.

Pergolas appear to be complicated, but they are relatively easy to build. Spec at least 2×6s for beams (the lowest, supportive element) or rafters (that stack atop beams or other rafters) that span up to 8 feet. Use at least 2×8s for beams or rafters of up to 11 feet in length. The pergolas *illustrated below* are just two possible configurations. Pergola designs vary according to the dimension of the lumber used, the number of rafter layers, the post treatment, and the type of decorative cut used on the ends of the members.

Beefing up the beams and rafters and matching the posts to those of the porch add a sense of substance and permanence to this pergola.

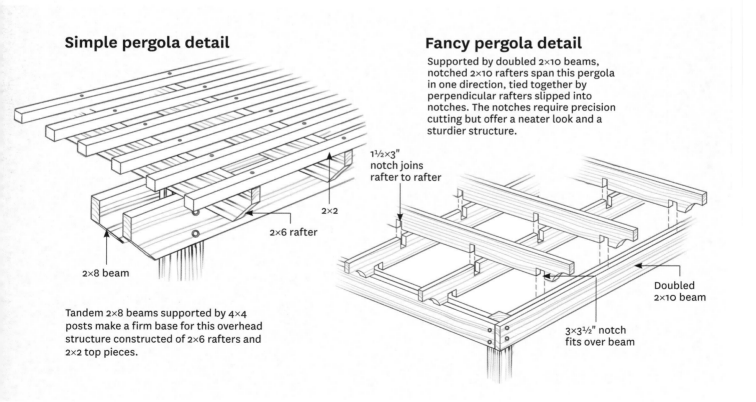

Simple pergola detail

2×2

2×6 rafter

2×8 beam

Tandem 2×8 beams supported by 4×4 posts make a firm base for this overhead structure constructed of 2×6 rafters and 2×2 top pieces.

Fancy pergola detail

Supported by doubled 2×10 beams, notched 2×10 rafters span this pergola in one direction, tied together by perpendicular rafters slipped into notches. The notches require precision cutting but offer a neater look and a sturdier structure.

1½×3" notch joins rafter to rafter

Doubled 2×10 beam

3×3½" notch fits over beam

Even a simple pergola
provides shade
and adds a graceful
transition to the
outdoors.

Entryway

Where you position the stairway is one way to signal an entryway. A handsome door, trim, and hardware treatment is another.

The simplest approach is painting the door a color that stands apart from the surrounding color scheme. You don't have to select a brash hue to create this effect—a solid block of contrasting color does the job. In a similar vein, moldings, such as pilasters and pediments, are classic design motifs that have been used for centuries to emphasize entryways.

A porch addition gives you an opportunity to replace the entry door or doors that lead from the porch into your home. Entry doors are available in a wide range of styles and types, providing a variety of design options. And because new technologies, materials, and manufacturing techniques have improved the performance of doors, you'll appreciate the smooth operation, weather-stripped fit, high-performance insulation, and attractive hardware choices a new door offers. And you have a wide range of materials to choose from (see *box below*).

Large porches and wraparound designs offer the possibility of adding a second entry door, a traditional feature of front porches. Plan second entryways carefully—they should be integrated with the interior design and configuration of your home. A door that

RIGHT: There's no doubt about where to find the entrance to this house. Doubling the posts adds visual variety. The lattice work is a pleasant echo of the sidelights flanking the door.

Material matters

Wood
- Energy efficient
- Requires periodic refinishing
- Swells and shrinks with humidity changes
- Preservative-treated wood offers maximum durability

Aluminum
- Virtually maintenance-free
- Cannot be planed, so installation must be exact
- Embossed covers and applied moldings mimic the characteristics of wood
- Many options offer foam core to slow heat transmission

Clad
- Combines the energy performance of wood with the low maintenance of engineered materials
- Cladding materials include metal, vinyl, and polyester

Fiberglass
- Superior energy efficiency
- Maintenance-free
- Accepts stain to mimic wood

Steel
- Virtually maintenance-free
- Cannot be planed, so installation must be exact
- Embossed covers and applied moldings offer characteristics of wood
- Many options offer foam core to slow heat transmission

Vinyl
- Superior energy efficiency
- Maintenance-free
- Accepts paint

A transom is an old
light-sharing technique
well worth reviving, for
both its functionality
and its good looks. If you
are adding a doorway
(see *page 137*), you may
find that the rim joist
above the door opening
substitutes for the
header.

Color, texture, and character

A porch doesn't have to relegate your entry door to the obscurity of shadows. Bring it forward by using contrasting colors on the door and trim. Doors of unusual shape or scale gain additional prominence if outlined in contrasting trim. Glass lets light reach indoors, but an additional value is its reflective quality, which grabs attention when viewed from outside. Decorative trim on screen doors can make them attention-getters too.

opens into your living or dining room will no doubt get extra use from active kids and pets with muddy feet. A better choice is to allow access to a kitchen or to create a private entry for a bedroom or home office. While you emphasize the location of your main entry, you'll probably want to de-emphasize the second, more secluded entry. Keep moldings and paint colors subtle. Remember that stairways leading directly to doors act as open invitations to approach. (For how to frame a second doorway, see *box opposite*.)

A centrally placed entry door bisects a large porch into two areas, establishing two separate outdoor living spaces. If you are planning a porch project and have the option of placing a front door in a number of locations, consider how you will use your porch. Placing the stairs and entry off to one side creates a large area for entertaining friends and family.

After you have decided the location of, general style of, and material for a new entry door leading from the porch indoors, consider glazing options such as frosted and beveled glass. Installing a door with glass panes will help to visually open the transition from the porch to inside your home. Transoms and sidelights are other options for reducing the visual barrier between a porch and the indoors.

The simplest upgrade for an entry is a well-chosen punch of color. If new hardware is in the budget as well, all the better.

Doors of unusual shape make for grand entries, but typically require new headers that will disrupt both interior and exterior wall surfaces.

Venturesome trim treatment pairs nicely with this out-of-the-ordinary Craftsman-influenced door. Enhancing the trim is fairly easy even if you don't redo the siding. Existing siding can always be cut away to accommodate new moldings.

Doorway framing

Once you have an idea of where you want a new doorway, check for obstructions. A quick look from the basement or crawlspace will tell you what's hidden inside the wall above. However, it's only when you cut into the wall that it will be clear whether wiring or plumbing has to be rerouted.

Support the joists above the opening with temporary bracing before removing any wall framing. A header of doubled 2×6s is strong enough for a 3-foot opening. If you are cutting a larger opening for a double door, heftier framing is necessary. You may choose to use an existing wall stud as a king stud, in which case you can cut the opening 1½ inches to the inside of that stud and slip a jack stud into the wall. After framing the opening, cut away the studs and bottom plate.

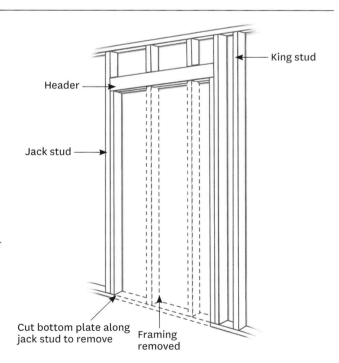

King stud

Header

Jack stud

Cut bottom plate along jack stud to remove

Framing removed

Walkways and landings

A brand-new porch deserves better than a cracked and tilting concrete walkway.

Walkways and landings offer an opportunity to provide contrasting color and texture to a porch. They also give you a chance to add some drama and variation with a winding or diagonal route.

The width of a walkway is best determined by its primary function. The walk that leads to your front door should be at least 4 feet wide to allow people to walk comfortably side by side. A secondary walkway need be only 2 to 3 feet wide. A tertiary path—one leading to a secluded garden area, for example—might only be 18 to 24 inches wide and made of simple crushed gravel.

Some walks are good do-it-yourself projects. Brick, stone, or pavers can be set on a sand base protected from weed incursion by a layer of landscaping fabric. For greater stability, set them in a concrete bed. Working with concrete is a job best left to the pros—smoothing and leveling takes experience, and when things go wrong, they can go wrong in a big way.

Brick pavers bordered by concrete make an attractive, long-lasting walkway that is relatively easy to clear of snow and ice. Because they are made of dense pressure-formed concrete, pavers are more durable than even formed concrete.

Purchasing tips

Stone is sold by the ton or square yard. Determine your walk's area or volume in advance so your supplier can convert your figures into the amount of stone you need. Stone is delivered on pallets.

Pavers are sold in quantity in banded cubes of about 90 square feet. Be prepared with the estimated total area of your walk. Order 5 to 10 percent more if your project requires a lot of cutting.

Brick is sold on pallets by the square yard. About 50 standard bricks cover a square yard of surface.

Tile is sold in cartons of varying amounts of square feet based on the thickness of the tile. Use only vitreous (non-absorbent) tile in cold climates.

Concrete is sold premixed by the cubic yard (27 cubic feet). That equates to a 4x20-foot walk that's 4 inches thick.

Loose stone is sold by the cubic yard or ton. Expect a ton of loose stone spread 1½ inches deep to cover about 17 square yards.

Choose SW-rated brick, made to withstand severe weather, including freeze-thaw cycles. For the same reasons, type M mortar or sand is used between bricks in walkways.

Combinations of pavers set in a sand and gravel bed make a good do-it-yourself project. The ability of sand and gravel beds to drain precipitation is an added benefit.

Flagstones—stone fractured or cleft into flat slabs 1½ inches thick—are set into sand or mortar for a relatively smooth finished surface. Slate, bluestone, limestone, redstone, sandstone, and granite are the most common types of rock used.

Wood or composite decking in a variety of forms makes a handsome walkway that drains rainfall quickly. However, in climates prone to year-round moss and mildew, it can be slippery.

Stone slab steps have an earthy drama and meld well with plantings. On the downside, they can be tricky to navigate and hard to remove snow and ice from. As a consequence, such steps are better suited to a secondary entrance.

Wiring

An outdoor living space like a porch needs all the lighting fixtures, switches, and receptacles that an indoor space does.

Installing the necessary cable and boxes is relatively simple to do before the floor and ceiling are installed. Your biggest challenge will be running circuits from the breaker box to the porch.

Many homeowners find that ceiling lights do a good job of general illumination but cast odd shadows. Wall-mounted fixtures bring the light down to human level, much the way floor and table lamps do indoors. Planning for plenty of receptacles, including some switched receptacles, gives ample scope for including floor and table lamps in your lighting scheme.

While wiring your porch, you have the opportunity to add motion-sensing security lights, hookups for low-voltage landscaping lighting, and receptacles for Christmas lighting. Bear in mind that wiring is one of those jobs that is simple when there is easy access for running conduit and cable but much more difficult after your porch is completed.

For your own safety and to avoid expensive redos later, obey your local codes. They will have special requirements regarding outdoor circuits, calling for either waterproof underground feed (UF) cable or conduit, or both. Receptacles must be ground fault circuit interrupter (GFCI) protected.

Unless you are experienced with wiring, it's best to hire a pro who can do this important job right and according to code. You may even find that your electrician will have some cost-saving suggestions well worth completing before closing in the construction.

Shown *opposite* are some common porch wiring situations. Black wires are hot, carrying power to the fixture. White wires are neutral, carrying power back to the panel. (In some wiring configurations, white wires are hot, in which case they must be marked with black marker or wrapped with electrical tape.) Red wires are also hot and used when a three-way switch is called for. A bare copper or green insulated wire is the ground.

ABOVE: Both ceiling fans and light fixtures require advance planning so cable and boxes can be installed before framing is covered. A porch offers a great opportunity for unusual light fixtures.

RIGHT: This Craftsman fixture is just one of many you can choose to suit the style of your porch. Its stained glass provides a warm, diffused light that can be supplemented by wall-mounted fixtures and table lamps.

End-line

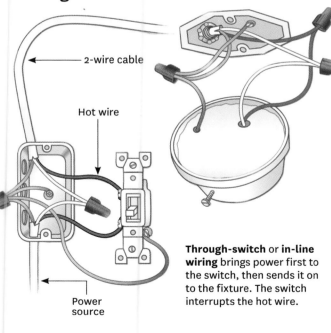

End-line or **switch-loop wiring** brings power first to the fixture. Two-wire cable running from the fixture to the switch creates a hot-wire loop that is interrupted by the switch.

Labels: White marked hot · 2-wire cable · Power source · White marked hot

Through-switch

Through-switch or **in-line wiring** brings power first to the switch, then sends it on to the fixture. The switch interrupts the hot wire.

Labels: 2-wire cable · Hot wire · Power source

Switched fixture and unswitched receptacle

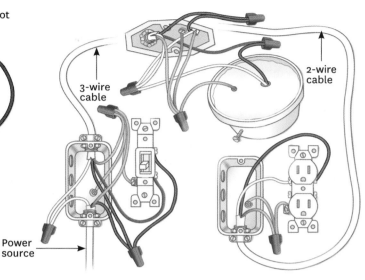

This switch, light, and receptacle arrangement has a **switched fixture** and an **unswitched receptacle**. Power comes into the switch box with two-wire cable. Three-wire cable carries power to the fixture; two-wire cable bears it on to the receptacle. The red wire carries power, interrupted by the switch to the light fixture. The black wire carries uninterrupted power to the receptacle.

Labels: 3-wire cable · 2-wire cable · Power source

GFCI receptacle

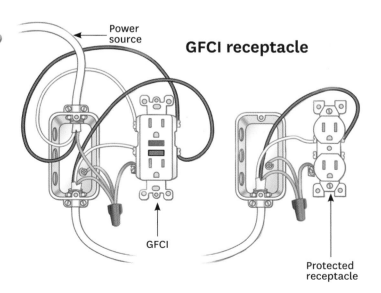

A ground fault circuit interrupter (GFCI) receptacle detects the slightest variation in current due to a shock or a short. Should it detect such a fault, it instantaneously shuts down the circuit. One GFCI can protect a series of standard receptacles downstream from the power source.

Labels: Power source · GFCI · Protected receptacle

the extras

For most people the word "porch" connotes rocking chairs, lemonade, and friendly waves to neighbors. And indeed, the classic front porch can be all of that. However, some porches offer more. With easy-to-change screens and windows, a **THREE-SEASON PORCH** can cope with spring and fall as well as summer—in some regions winter too. Add a sink to your grilling area and you have the beginnings of an **OUTDOOR KITCHEN**. And if you enjoy gathering around a fire, consider adding the focus and warmth of a **FIREPLACE**. Each of these options takes some planning and will have a significant effect on your budget. This chapter provides some great ideas for enhancing porches and essential information for what it takes to add these extras on. You'll also learn what alternatives you have for achieving a porch "extra" without breaking the bank.

Kitchen areas

Adding a cooking area to your porch can be as simple as carving out a safe spot for a grill and incorporating a bit of counter space.

Or it can grow to a full-blown kitchen including a grill fed by natural gas, a sink with hot and cold water, a refrigerator, a wine cooler area, and plenty of cabinets. Elaborate kitchens typically appear on porches in regions where the temperatures are moderate and the livin' is easy at least three seasons of the year. However, the allure of outdoor cooking is so strong that even in the Midwest and Northeast homeowners are choosing to add outdoor kitchens to their porches.

As you work out the budget for a kitchen area, you'll find a surprising range of costs. Dependable stand-alone grills run from $300 for a basic

ABOVE: With enough shelter, standard wood cabinets work well, though in high-humidity areas avoid units made of veneer over particleboard or chipboard cores.

RIGHT: A stand-alone grill with a simple cabinet and counter setup equips you for summertime cooking.

OPPOSITE: Stainless-steel access cabinets set into stonework can help you cook up a storm and withstand any weather.

model up to $1,000 or more for one with additional features. A drop-in grill suitable for setting into a countertop costs from $1,500 up to $4,200. Likewise, an outdoor compact fridge or wine cooler can cost as little as a few hundred dollars or as much as several thousand. Stainless-steel cabinets and drawers are the best bet if there is a chance of rain blowing in. For access cabinet doors, plan on $100 to $400; access drawers cost $200 to $500.

For 6 feet of tiled countertop, budget about $500, installed. (Be sure to spec all-weather tile.) If your porch is near supply sources, figure about $800 to run hot and cold water lines and a drain line. To avoid having to replace propane tanks (and occasionally be caught with no propane to cook with), have a gas line run from your house to the grill for about $600.

Design an outdoor kitchen as thoughtfully as an indoor kitchen to maximize both usability and enjoyment.

WHAT IT TAKES
Plumbing basics

Adding a permanent kitchen to your porch involves some plumbing. Costs will vary based on the difficulty of running plumbing lines to your porch. The essentials include hot and cold water lines, a drain line tying into your household drain system, and a natural gas line. If code permits, you may be able to save the cost of a drain and use a dry well instead. The well, made of a plastic container filled with stones, holds waste water and slowly percolates the "gray water" into the surrounding soil. If your hot water line must run a long way from your water heater, consider installing an on-demand water heater (about $400).

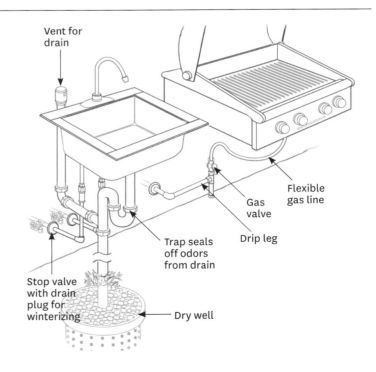

Vent for drain

Flexible gas line

Gas valve

Drip leg

Trap seals off odors from drain

Stop valve with drain plug for winterizing

Dry well

Fireplace

If a fireplace in a porch strikes you as a mad attempt to heat the outdoors, think back to the joys of gathering around a campfire as night falls.

Add a fireplace to your porch and you've not only added a great focal point, but you've also made the porch a magnet area for entertaining even in the cooler shoulder seasons.

In addition, you'll find that the inevitable mess of having a fireplace—hauling logs in, toting ashes out—is a lot easier to handle on a porch.

Costs can range from about $4,000 for a professionally installed prefab metal firebox in fireplacelike casing to $20,000 or more for a full-blown stone or brick fireplace. The prefab option

ABOVE: Whether cast-stone veneer or the real thing, the look of field stone is great for a porch fireplace.

LEFT: A fireplace can be the whole point of a porch. Centered on a brick fireplace, this porch redefines outdoor living.

can look better than you might think, especially with the addition of highly realistic manufactured stone veneer. Though somewhat more costly, cast stone mantels add the look of sculpted stone. Made of crushed stone or aggregate, cast stone comes in several naturalistic colors, does not require a foundation, and is just as fireproof as the real thing.

The high cost of real masonry is not just labor and material. Due to the extreme weight of the installation, you'll need to have a foundation added just for the fireplace—a costly add-on when the rest of the porch requires only concrete piers spaced every few feet.

ABOVE: Even in the summer, a fireplace is an attractive feature

RIGHT: The traditional appeal of the brick fireplace is a handsome companion to the grill alcove next to it.

ABOVE: An alcove can be a handy place for storing firewood.

LEFT: Precast stone can be remarkably light, often requiring minimal structural bracing.

How firm a foundation

The cost and complexity of adding a fireplace to your porch depends on the type of fireplace you want. The three options shown here all deliver a live flame from real wood but require varying degrees of structural preparation. For example, a masonry fireplace will need a full foundation to handle its massive weight. A prefab metal firebox and chimney with a cast stone or drywall surround is much lighter, needing a pier or two to shore up the floor joists. A freestanding fireplace generally needs no additional support at all.

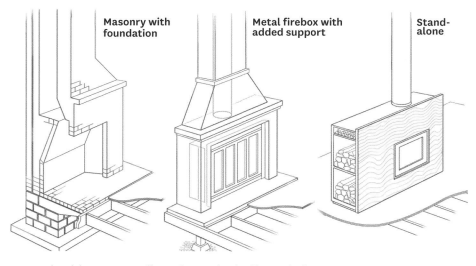

Masonry with foundation

Metal firebox with added support

Stand-alone

Floor joists vary according to the span involved but typically are 2×6s or 2×8s spaced 16 inches apart. A masonry fireplace with its foundation is virtually a freestanding structure with floor joists surrounding it. A metal firebox with a surround needs minimal added support. A stand-alone sits directly on the floor.

Screened and three-season porches

Installing screens and storm windows as the seasons change greatly extends the usefulness of your porch.

Planning for screens and windows in advance will save you money and result in a better looking porch.

Not only can you have the supporting posts built or milled to accept screens and storms, but you can have decorative insets made to suit the style of your porch. When planning, bear in mind that the maximum width of screen is 7 feet. However, sticking to a maximum width of 4 feet is best to avoid sagging. (See *page 118* for more on screens.) Take advantage of the various types of screen available:

• Pet-proof screen is ideal for lower panels if you have a rambunctious beast.
• Fine mesh screen of 20×20 wires per inch (18×18 is standard) fends off gnats.
• Fine strands preserve your view.

WHAT IT TAKES
Prefab advantage

Screens and storm windows can be custom made after your porch is constructed, but prefabbing them speeds installation and better assures that screens, storms, and decorative inserts will fit accurately. The arrangement *shown at right* starts with a prefabbed wall frame. The screens and storms and the decorative inserts are built in the shop or factory to suit the frame, saving on-site time and labor. As posts and overhead beams go up, each wall frame is installed. It's then an easy job to install the screens or storms and the decorative inserts. Removing screens and adding storm windows is done from the inside with no tramping on the flower beds.

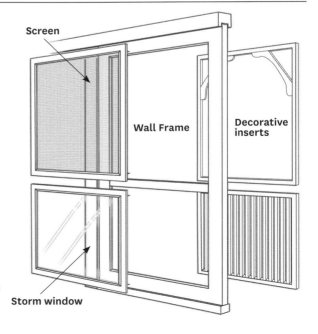

Screen

Wall Frame

Decorative inserts

Storm window

THIS PAGE: Double-hung windows with screens and shades have this vibrant porch ready for anything.

OPPOSITE: Far from an afterthought, the decorative treatment in the gable squares with the positioning of the post.

details

Selecting the finishing touches for your porch can be a real pleasure. We've assembled a variety of details to consider. **ARCHITECTURAL ELEMENTS** like exposed rafters and corbels ring in the new by echoing the old. The reverse can be true as well; a new porch provides a great opportunity to add architectural detail to an otherwise featureless home. **DOORS** can cost as much as your wallet can bear, but keep in mind that even a modest-priced door sporting the right accent color—and some decent hardware—can do the job very well. Don't overlook the value of good **HARDWARE:** Substance, style, and security are the stuff of a quality entry lockset. Stylish mail slots, house numbers, and doorknockers add refinement. New **LIGHTS AND FANS** extend the use of your porch. Whatever the weather, you can increase your **COMFORT** on an open porch with heaters and misters. Finally, consider **PLANTERS** to unify your porch and landscape.

Architectural elements

A few well-chosen architectural elements can make all the difference in a porch.

In many builder homes, the fascia is un-exceptional, and the roofing is standard-issue composite shingles. Yet with the addition of a set of elegantly tapered columns, for example, the house becomes a thing of beauty. When budgeting, allow a little extra for built-in features that make a difference.

The right architectural elements have lifted many a blank builder's special to a new plane of existence. The trick is finding a glimmer of style in it, then amplifying it with some expressive elements. And it's not all just for looks. As you'll find in the following pages, the careful choice of apron material, railings, and even a window or two can make a functional difference as well.

ABOVE: Carefully worked corbels and beaded board help an arched overhang live big, a pleasing contrast to the rough-hewn cedar siding beside it.

LEFT: For a cost-effective alternative to standard dimensional lumber, consider composite materials. SmartTrim, shown here, is made of resin-locked wood fiber and is easy to work, stable, and long-lasting.

RIGHT: Need a windbreak or a touch of privacy? Hanging a lattice panel or two gets the job done without being heavy-handed.

What's more inviting than a porch done right? This gem has all the elements—a vaulted planked ceiling, Herculean columns, and lovely railings. It scores on the details as well, with color, texture, and blissful comforts.

A beaded-board ceiling, gracious columns, classic wicker, and relaxed fabrics. . . . Can't you just feel the gentle breeze rolling through this perfect porch? It's all attainable.

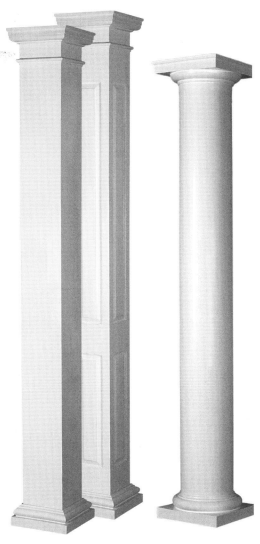

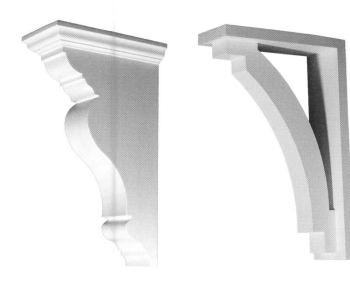

ABOVE LEFT: Windows have a place in a porch, especially to provide shelter from prevailing winds. These open wide and don't hinder the view.

ABOVE RIGHT: Columns made of composite materials and fiberglass resist warping, cracking, and deterioration. Make this decision early in your planning; framing needs to be planned around the exact height of the column. You can find these at Pacific Columns (pacificcolumns.com).

LEFT: These decorative brackets (they are almost never truly structural) are made of high-density foam that is easy to work with and long lasting. These are from Apex Millwork (apexmillwork.net).

Doors

An entry door that shows the ravages of too many comings and goings does your new porch no favors.

If the budget is tight, fresh paint and a new lockset can do wonders—but to really complete the package, consider a new door.

While the door itself will be one of the last things you'll install, plan for it early. You may want to include new trim, which will affect your siding. You may even decide to go with a larger door, which will mean framing changes that alter interior and exterior finishes. Think ahead on your lockset choice as well; some require cutouts other than the usual pre-drilled openings that doors come with. Consider your storm door too; it will be the first thing people see. If you want to show off your entry door, consider a "full view" storm.

RIGHT: Stained glass is just the sort of hand-wrought touch a Craftsman door calls for. This one is by Floating World Wood Design (perceptionofdoors.com).

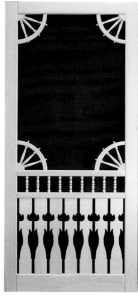

FAR LEFT: Sliding doors are handy for side or back porches. Shown here is the Frenchwood Gliding Patio Door from Andersen (andersenwindows.com).

CENTER LEFT: Stile-and-rail construction incorporating glass with an asymmetrical design is squarely in the Craftsman tradition. The Four Square Door is from Simpson Door (simpsondoor.com).

LEFT: Nothing says summer quite like the slam of a wooden screen door. Trimmed out in Victorian fashion, this screen door is from Coppa Woodworking (coppawoodworking.com).

Sidelights and an overhead fanlight increase interior light and beautifully enhance an entryway. If you are upgrading from a standard-width door, you'll need to remove exterior siding to reframe the opening. Pictured is the 400 Series KML Entranceway by Andersen (andersenwindows.com).

Hardware

A finely finished porch deserves all those bits of hardware that give a quality finish to a project.

A little web browsing will uncover an amazing array of items that suit the style of your porch—and probably several you didn't realize you needed. But be prepared for sticker shock: Buying a good lockset with matching hinges, a period mailbox, and stylish house numbers may set you back the better part of a thousand dollars.

If some items are not in the budget right now, less expensive substitutes can stand in while you save for the ones you really want. Some appealing details, like a kickplate or doorknocker, can be late additions.

If you plan to keep an existing door, measure the backset—the distance from the center of the knob to the edge of the door. For exterior doors, 2¾ inches is typical and will suit standard locksets. However, if you have a hefty mortise lock in mind, your door will require some skilled joinery.

Most of these items are quick to install once you decide where to place them. Place an item like a mailbox or a set of house numbers on a piece of paper and trace around it. As you do so, mark the location of any mounting screws. Cut out the silhouettes and tape them in place to evaluate where they'll be most effective. When you've settled on a spot, use the cutouts to guide drilling holes for the fasteners.

ABOVE: The gleam of bright brass hardware and the sheen of a colorful door make this entryway the focal point of a front porch.

RIGHT: Victorian in spirit, this Chinese-Chippendale pattern dates from the 1880s. Measuring 11¼ inches wide by 3½ inches high, this mail slot is cast from brass using the lost wax process. It's from House of Antique Hardware (houseofantique.com).

RIGHT: This selection of bright brass hardware from Schlage (consumer.schlage.com) demonstrates the power of assembling matching items.

LEFT: The beauty of bronze is that its patina alters with age. This handcrafted door set is part of the Rustic Revival line of exterior door hardware from Taamba Hardware (taamba.com).

LEFT: If your home is your castle, you'll like the armorlike construction of the solid brass Roland mailbox, suited for Classical Revival homes of the 1920s and '30s. Available from Rejuvenation (rejuvenation.com).

BELOW: Born of a shipboard need for sturdy hardware that stows out of the way, this latch is ideal for access panels in a porch floor or cabinets. This flush ring pull is from Baldwin Hardware (baldwinhardware.com).

Lights and fans

The simple promise, "We'll leave the porch light on," has beckoned many a weary traveler home.

An illuminated porch gets right to the heart of a warm and homey welcome. However, getting the lighting right takes some doing.

First of all, think beyond the ceiling fixture. It is a great staple, but left to its own devices casts unattractive shadows on people's faces, creates an unpleasant glare, and is impossible for reading. Better is a combination of fixtures, with sconces and lanterns that are positioned low enough to bring light down to human level. Entry lights flanking the entryway, *as shown at right*, mark the front door as the point of entry, help illuminate the steps and landing, and add a decorative touch. Ceiling-mounted can lights help eliminate shadowy corners.

When designed right, effective lighting doesn't always stand out—it simply works. Ask friends with porches what they like and don't like about their porch illumination. And consult with your electrician. You'll learn about the options available and how to break up circuits so you can easily switch on only the lights you need. Here are some great lights and fans to help you start planning.

RIGHT: The Schoolhouse ceiling fan has classic details. From The Period Arts Fan Company (periodarts.com).

WHAT IT TAKES
Fastening fans

Most municipal codes require that ceiling fans have a special box that is strong enough to handle the oscillation of the fan's blades. This is not something you want to scrimp on. Fan-rated boxes, made of steel or high-impact plastic, attach directly to a ceiling joist. An alternative is a fan-rated metal bracket that fits between the joists, a good option if you don't have a joist running exactly where you want to position your fan.

Put light at human level with sconces and lanterns that illuminate without blinding.

ABOVE LEFT: UL listed for damp locations, the Chicago Flush Mount is 12 inches wide and made of cast aluminum. From Kichler Lighting (kichler.com).

ABOVE RIGHT: The Prairie by Progress Lighting (progresslighting.com) comes in brushed nickel, speckled brown, or speckled black finishes.

LEFT: These entry lights come with Waterglass lanterns that create a shimmering effect. On the upper porch, simple can lights provide subtle illumination that doesn't detract from the main-floor lighting scheme. All lights from Progress Lighting (progresslighting.com).

Comfort

Exposed to the elements, most porches must take weather as it comes. However, with a few well-chosen items, you can enjoy your porch throughout the warm seasons.

To defeat the broiling days of August, consider adding shades. Made of all-weather fabric that blocks ultra-violet rays, roll-down sunshades installed on the sunny side of your porch still let some of the breeze through.

If you live in an intensely hot and dry region, consider installing misters. Powered by a pump, nozzles spray a very fine mist to cool the air by means of flash evaporation. Misters are friends to plants and people alike.

When there is a chill in the air, infrared heaters warm people and objects without wasting energy heating the air. Powered by standard 120-volt current, they can be wall-mounted or hung from the ceiling.

ABOVE: Comfort is more than just a pleasant temp and protection from the elements. Cushy furniture can make all the difference.

BELOW: The chaise has evolved in many directions since the Victorian classic on "sleeping porches" of the past. Whatever form it takes, a chaise always invites one to linger.

WHAT IT TAKES
Weather wiring

Use an outdoor-rated fixture for anything that will be directly exposed to rain, sleet, or snow. Allow for wind-blown precipitation. For fixtures tucked into a vaulted ceiling or wall-mounted yards away from the weather, interior fixtures can be used. However, be aware that they may corrode more quickly because they are out of the controlled indoor climate they were intended for. If in doubt, consult with a lighting retailer or your electrician, or go directly to the manufacturer.

ABOVE LEFT: Styled like a table lamp but made to comfortably heat a 12-foot-diameter area, the Endless Summer New Orleans lamp from Blue Rhino (bluerhino .com) has an automatic shutoff switch should it be knocked over.

ABOVE RIGHT: These sunshades by Coolaroo (coolaroousa.com) roll up when not in use. When needed, they block UV rays while letting in airflow and permitting porch users a bit of a view outside.

LEFT: Permanent mister installations such as this one from Rapid Cool (rapidcool .net) use stainless-steel piping equipped with nozzles every foot or so. Pumps to run water through the system can be installed in a garage or other outbuilding.

Planters

Your porch will look even more inviting with the color and softening influence of plants.

That means containers: pots, baskets, brackets, and window boxes. Container gardening is hugely popular and very rewarding. Keep in mind that containers require drainage to cope with intense rain and over watering. A piece of landscaping fabric in the bottom of a pot filters dirt from the run off. A layer of gravel on top of the fabric and beneath the soil acts as a moisture reservoir. To avoid damage to your porch floor, use saucers or clay pot feet beneath containers.

Containers need frequent water in hot weather. Watering plants daily can be an enjoyable ritual, but a micro-irrigation system with a timer assures regular watering and is especially convenient for out-of-reach plants.

To nourish your plants, buy potting soil with time-release fertilizer. Add water-soluble fertilizer once a week, tapering off at the end of the season.

To attract butterflies, add such plants and flowers as ageratum, aster, bluebeard, cosmos, petunias, purple coneflower, Russian sage, sweet alyssum, and zinnia. To attract hummingbirds, plant cardinal climber, culinary sage, cypress vine, daylilies, fuchsias, and honeysuckles.

Buying annuals for containers is an enjoyable rite of spring, but some perennials also do well in confinement. In sunny areas consider perennial fountain grass, hardy chrysanthemum, lamb's-ears, creeping verbena, and yucca. In shade, choose from coral bells, astilbe, Japanese painted fern, bergenia, and variegated Japanese sedge.

ABOVE: Simple wire baskets filled with sphagnum moss are ideal accents. With time, the plants will envelope the baskets to become true hanging gardens. Some gardeners insert plants into the sides of the basket to enhance the lushness of the arrangement.

LEFT: Don't neglect the railing, an accessible area ideal for kitchen herbs as well as decorative plants.

OPPOSITE: Climbing ivy can become part of the porch itself. Limit it to masonry to avoid moisture damage.

Paint

The quintessential finishing touch, painting should be great fun, but too often it leads to angst about what colors are right. Here are some ways to choose color with confidence.

Use color combos recommended by paint companies. That may seem unimaginative, but often you can find color selections that suit your taste and avoid expensive, time-consuming mistakes. At the very least, the combos provide a solid starting point.

Complement the neighborhood. You don't have to totally blend in, but avoid harsh contrast. Stand out in a subtle, unobtrusive way.

Let your porch furnishings provide the accent colors. Because porches are viewed face-on, boldly colored chairs and settees pack a lot of punch.

Define the entry with color on the door—perhaps the stair risers as well.

Play off elements of your house with those colors that are pretty much givens, such as masonry and roofing. Don't leave them out of your color scheme—they make more of an impact than you might think. (If new roofing is part of your plans, consider neutrals like white, gray, and black, and variegated combos that don't inhibit porch color choices.)

Tiny paint swatches are notoriously misleading. Make the minor investment in several sample jars of paint. Slap the colors right on the house where you can see the effect of sun and shade. Once you've made your choice, don't skimp on the prep. Granted, all that scraping, repairing, and priming is the least pleasant aspect of painting, but it is the foundation of a crisp, long-lasting paint job (see box, *opposite*, for more preparation details). Finally, heed the manufacturer's recommendations about the right temperatures and weather conditions for painting.

Skip the chip— buy sample jars of appealing colors and test them right where you plan to use them.

RIGHT: Manufacturer's paint combinations are a handy starting point for paint selection. Buying samples and painting large swatches on your porch is by far the best way to evaluate colors.

Victorian-style homes traditionally have many colors. Three, maybe four, colors make an eye-catching combination. More than that can be overwhelming.

Painting tips

If your porch is part of a whole-house upgrade, painting will entail a wide range of preparation chores:

• Rinse away surface dirt, then use detergent and a brush to remove grime. Or use trisodium phosphate (TSP), a degreaser that etches old paint for better adhesion.

• Repair small areas of rot by scraping the area and removing rotten wood. Prep the cavity with liquid epoxy, then apply epoxy filler. Smooth with a rasp, then sand the area.

• Replace sections of siding, sills, or trim if the damage is extensive.

• Pry out any loose caulk and recaulk. Make sure all joints are caulked.

• Prep new wood with paintable preservative.

• Equip yourself with canvas drop cloths (they absorb paint instead of letting it puddle) and quality brushes.

• Spray painting is quick and ideal for complex architectural elements, but coverage does not last as long.

• Be orderly. Minimize spatter where you don't want it by painting in this sequence: ceiling, siding, trim, railings, and floor.

case studies

Building a porch involves a variety of skills ranging from the grunt work of pier digging to the finesse of fine carpentry. In fact, a porch is a **HOUSE IN MINIATURE**, requiring several disciplines that assure the structure will withstand the test of time. That means a serious foundation that keeps the porch from sagging, flooring that will bear up under all sorts of weather, rock-solid stairs and railings, and a sheltering roof. This chapter chronicles the **CONSTRUCTION OF THREE PORCHES**, offering a time-lapse portrayal of how things come together. If you hire a contractor, this chapter gives you a good idea of what to expect on your job site. If you are building your porch yourself, you may discover some vital tricks of the trade that will **SAVE YOU TIME AND MONEY**—and boost the quality of your work. You'll also gain valuable insights on some of the challenges of porch building and a realistic look at what to expect.

before

ABOVE: Weary aluminum siding was one of the first things to go before porch construction began. The original lap siding underneath was patched where possible, replaced when necessary. The finished porch is a welcoming centerpiece on a corner lot near the historic town center of Downers Grove, Illinois.

Queen Anne wraparound

When Jim and Robin Krusenoski contacted architect Cinda Lester, they knew they wanted an expansive, welcoming front porch for their 1894 home. "This is a front porch type of neighborhood," explains Lester. "Jim and Robin wanted a front porch not just for curb appeal, they really wanted some outdoor living space." And because the couple is highly involved in local historical preservation, they wanted the porch to be well crafted and in keeping with local housing stock.

The porch, part of a remodel that included a second-story addition and interior upgrades, was the capstone of the project. It had to meet tight setback requirements and be a welcoming presence on two streets. It's a great example of what it takes to build a quintessential American front porch—a porch that lives big and looks great.

1 Local building code required trenching 42 inches below grade before pouring the footing for the foundation wall. In the meantime, a simple T brace made of 2x6s supports the roof.

2 A new 8-inch foundation does the same job as the home's original 18-inch-thick limestone foundation. The homeowners hoped to salvage as much of the old porch as possible, but the floor was too far gone to save.

3 As the floor frame takes shape, a short wall of 2x6s supports 2x8 floor joists. The builder, Joe Corcoran, opted for pressure-treated lumber in the perimeter wall: "We knew it was going to be exposed to the most potential splash, ice, snow—all the seasonal changes. We just wanted to be sure."

WHAT IT TAKES
Cold-weather cure

An early snow and temperatures below freezing called for an insulated tarp to protect the concrete while it cured. Below grade, rigid foam insulates an area where the basement was expanded.

4 RIGHT: A load-bearing beam of Laminated Veneer Lumber (LVL) runs across the front of the porch and into the gazebo corner.

5 BELOW: Temporary 2x4 posts support the porch roof during the rough and tumble of construction; turned posts come later. "Typically the porch railing is absolutely the last thing to go on," says Lester. "You don't want it to get damaged."

WHAT IT TAKES
Whose job is it?

Complex structures like the gazebo roof pose a problem for architects—do they micromanage the framing or hand it over to the builder? Architect Cinda Lester chose the latter course: "The architect has to decide: How much do we need to dimension and detail, and how much do we just let the contractor know that this is what we want it to look like?" Complex features always need a little bit of "field customization," says contractor Joe Corcoran. For instance, as framing began, it was clear that for visual effect the gazebo roof should be pitched a bit higher. Now it's perfect.

6 Load-bearing posts tie into the floor joists and, wherever possible, sit directly on the wall framing. Priming the lower areas of the post in advance was an extra precaution. "We even had the painter prime the entire underside of the porch," says Corcoran.

7 The homeowners opted for fir flooring that would be in keeping with their century-old home. The tongues and grooves got a coat of preservation before installation. To handle drainage, the floor slants away from the house ¼ inch for every 12 inches.

8 Short posts are tied into the framing, one to support a secondary stairway railing, the other where railings meet in a corner.

9 With posts in place and the roof readied for shingles, the profile of the new porch becomes clear.

10 With the roofing on, snowstorms can do their worst and the porch is protected. The porch doubles as a staging area for building materials used in the interior of the home. Construction paper protects the flooring.

11 New 3-inch-to-the-weather cedar siding covers walls on the addition and is patched in where the old siding is too far gone. Any nail holes and minor blemishes are filled and primed before painting.

12 Code requires a maximum of 4 inches between the narrowest profile of the balusters. Railing sections of 2x6 cedar are assembled on the floor before they are trimmed to fit and installed.

13 As with any construction project, the finished stairs are the last thing to go in. Otherwise, the coming and going of materials is bound to damage the treads and railings.

14 With the walls painted, the beaded-board tongue-and-groove ceiling goes on. The stairway from the gazebo leads to a pool area in a side yard. The homeowners wanted a smooth surface under the eaves. Birch plywood fit the bill.

15 The apron is functional as well as ornamental: It lets the porch breathe. "The homeowners knew they didn't want off-the-shelf home-center lattice," says Lester. Getting the right stuff within budget called for innovation (see "Innovation pays").

16 Setback restrictions required a notch in a corner of the porch. ("We tried and tried for a variance," says Lester.) In the end, the corner had to be an innie, not an outie, and looks great. The tandem stairways welcome visitors from either side of the corner lot.

WHAT IT TAKES
Innovation pays

An online supplier listed the cutouts for the porch apron at $35 a piece—a budget breaker. The do-it-yourself approach was pricey too: "We tried to cut the pieces with a jigsaw and it took us an hour just to cut one," says Corcoran. Instead, he turned to a stone-cutting company with a computerized water jet saw used to make fine cuts in granite. The machine cut the pieces out of SmartTrim, a wood fiber and resin product. The cost using the water jet? Just $11 per piece.

ABOVE: Cultured stone on the column bases and the porch apron is in keeping with the Craftsman tradition of mixing media. "People turn up their nose at the idea of cultured stone," says Cinda Lester, architect on the project. "When they actually see it, they change their minds."

Well-crafted Craftsman

Why was an expansive porch such a priority for Pete and Peggy Tomchek? "It sounds kind of lame, but we're just front-porch kind of people," laughs Pete. The Tomcheks chose to build a Craftsman-style home to suit their older suburban Chicago neighborhood. That meant deep eaves, stickwork in the gables, and a generous porch with hallmark Craftsman columns. The Tomcheks also sought to rein in their carbon footprint, buying salvaged doors for the interior and recycled steel railings for the porch and keeping construction waste to a minimum. The resulting porch exceeded their expectations. "We love it," says Pete. "It fits us, and it fits our neighborhood."

1 To keep the front of the house open, a laminated 2×10 beam carries the roof load. The total span for the front of the porch is 24 feet.

2 Tripled 2×6s form the structural core of the columns. Running from the foundation to the laminated beam, they bear the load of the roof and are more than adequate to support the porch railings.

3 The 2×10 floor joists placed 16 inches on center "are probably a bit over-engineered," says Tomchek, but he wanted the floor to be rock solid. Blocking, the short pieces placed between the joists, keep the members from twisting.

WHAT IT TAKES
Support masonry

Masonry veneer must be set on a completely stable base. Any give at all can crack the mortar and compromise the installation, good reason to add extra blocking to stiffen the rim joist.

4 An inset, secondary stairway called for special framing. The stairs are set back into the porch to keep them from projecting too near a neighbor's property. "It wasn't a code issue," says Tomchek. "We just didn't want things too tight."

5 Simple OSB (Oriented Strand Board) stiffened by 2×4s make up the substructure for the column bases. Laminated blocks of cedar 2×6s, glued and fastened with deck screws, provide a stable spot for attaching the railings.

6 It took some agonizing to decide the height and girth of the columns' bases—something that is hard to judge and is often one of the last decisions made. Plywood along the skirting is attached to the 2×6 frame, a stable base for the cultured stone. Because an ice and water shield covers the plywood, pressure-treated material wasn't necessary.

7 After installing wood decking, gapped for drainage, the scratch coat of mortar goes on over steel mesh, meeting the concrete foundation near grade level. The secondary stairway is installed, save for the railing. The homeowner incorporated many salvaged items in the construction of the home, including most of the steel railings. The wood fastening points for the railing are masked to keep them clear of mortar.

8 Cultured stone wraps each column, starting with the corners. Foam insulation spacers flex with the variation in the stone pieces. Tomchek points out that the materials cost for cultured stone is higher than for conventional stone, but it requires less labor and a less substantial foundation. Overall, it is a budget saver.

9 A second coat of mortar goes on as the stones are applied. The art of installing cultured stone is varying the size and color of the pieces to look like natural variations.

10 A local welder fabricated additional railing sections to match those the Tomcheks bought from a salvage yard.

11 To avoid having to scribe the flooring around the column bases, the cultured stone pieces are installed after the flooring.

12 Once the railing is cut to exact length, clips are fastened in a groove that runs along the top and bottom of the railing. Bolts are fastened through the clips to hold the railing to the column base.

13 Though cast concrete would have fit the bill, Tomchek choose Indiana limestone for capstones because of its beauty and durability. The limestone arrives cut to size. The notch for the column core is cut on-site.

14 Mortared in place, the limestone tops off the masonry beautifully. Waterproof caulk sealant protects the joint from moisture.

15 Stairway railings are always a difficult part of any porch project. This one required custom-cut baluster pieces set in holes bored in the flooring and steps.

16 Made from ¾-inch cedar plywood, the tapered columns are trimmed with 1× cedar. Gray ice and water shield wraps the bottom of the column. As a final step, 1×4 trim will cover the shield material.

18 Venting keeps the interior of the soffit free of moisture.

17 Stained to a rich brown and sealed, the cedar flooring contrasts nicely with the painted siding and naturally finished ceiling. Tomchek chose to use 12-foot cedar planks that abut a plank set perpendicularly in the middle of the porch. "I just liked the look of it breaking it up," he says. Hidden fasteners hold the planks and maintain a consistent gap for drainage.

before

ABOVE: Paired columns team up with a small pergola to add architectural interest and space for climbing plants. "We tried to bring some depth to the front of the home," says Rosario Ungaro, builder on the project.

Bungalow upgrade

This Toronto ranch-bungalow was so homely it was slated for demolition. But neighbors resisted plans to replace the 1950s home with four townhouses, so it sat empty—for years. Then, a newly retired couple recognized its potential. Not only was the home located in the coveted Hyde Park area of Toronto, it offered a great site. "Outside the front door is a wonderful playground where the whole neighborhood congregates," says builder Rosario Ungaro of Benchmark Building Services. "There is also a stream. The location was to die for." Ungaro teamed up with landscape designer Connie Cadotte of Garden Retreats to come up with a porch-pergola combo. It added depth and interest without breaking the budget—and helps the bungalow live up to its location.

1 The concrete landing needed resurfacing but was fundamentally in good shape, so simple piers were all that was needed for the new columns. Toronto's frigid winters call for 48-inch-deep footings.

2 Frames of pressure-treated 2×6 lumber form the bases of the new columns. A bottom plate, fastened to the footing with ½-inch anchor bolts, is overlapped by the frame so the two sides will be firmly joined.

3 To complete the corner, a second 2×6 frame is fastened to the 2×6 bottom plate, then attached to the larger frame.

4 Ungaro chose sign-painting board—an exterior plywood with a smooth resin finish—to give the bases a finished surface. Cedar tops them off.

5 With the bases roughed in, the 6×6 cedar posts go up. A 2×6 top plate, the first step in building the overhead frieze, ties them together.

6 A second 2×6 upper plate faced with ¾-inch exterior plywood completes the casing of the frieze. Pine crown molding tops it off. Next, the frieze is wired for small puck lights.

7 To finish off the structure, cedar 1×3s trim out the frieze. The concrete landing gets a new stone surface.

8 The columns are also detailed with trim. "Believe it or not, there are 105 different pieces to those columns," says Ungaro. Two 2x10 beams, prepainted by the homeowner, form the basis for the pergola.

9 LEFT: The topmost cross members sit on the two beams, providing plenty of shade without having to be tied into the house. The house is relatively tall for a one-story, but the picture window runs up to the eaves, necessitating the wraparound framing for the pergola.

10 ABOVE: With the carpentry complete, the bungalow has new-found style.

11 Painting brings life to the rich detail of the trim.

12 A shallow pergola over the garage balances the effect of the entryway treatment. Coated only with preservative, the top members of the pergolas contrast with the color of the posts and beams.

A–B

Actual dimension. True size of a piece of lumber. See also *Nominal dimension*.

Backbutter. To apply mortar or adhesive to a brick or the rear face of a tile before setting it.

Backerboard. Any of several cement or gypsum-based sheets used as substrate for setting tile. Also called cement board.

Balusters. Spindles that help support a staircase handrail.

Batten. A narrow strip of wood used to cover joints between boards or panels.

Beam. In framing, a horizontal support member.

Bearing wall. An interior or exterior wall that helps support the roof or the floor joists above.

Bevel cut. A cut through the thickness of a piece of wood at other than a 90-degree angle.

Blind-nail. To nail so that the head of the nail is not visible on the surface of the wood.

Board. Any piece of lumber that is less than 2 inches thick and more than 3 inches wide.

Board foot. The standard unit of measurement for wood. One board foot is equal to a piece 12×12×1 inches (nominal size).

Building code. Local ordinance governing the manner in which a home may be constructed or modified. Most codes are concerned with fire and health, with separate sections relating to electrical, plumbing, and structural work.

Butt joint. The joint formed by two pieces of material when fastened end to end, end to face, or end to edge.

C

Cantilever. A beam or beams projecting beyond a support member.

Casing. Trim around a door, window, or other opening.

Caulk. Any compound used to seal seams and joints against infiltration of water and air.

Chalkline. A reel of string coated with colored chalk, used to mark straight lines by pulling the string taught and snapping it. Also the line left by such a string.

Chamfer. A bevel cut made along the length of a board edge.

Clinch. To hammer the exposed tip of a nail at an angle, bending its point into the surrounding wood for added joint strength.

Code. See *Building code*.

Composition shingles. Roofing shingles with a felt or fiberglass base treated with asphalt and covered with mineral granules. These are the most common roofing material.

Concrete. A building and paving material made by mixing water with sand, gravel, and cement.

Concrete nails. Hardened-steel nails that can be driven into concrete.

Counterflashing. Pieces of flashing that cover other flashings to provide a more weatherproof seal.

Course. A row of shingles or other roofing or horizontal siding. Roofing and horizontal siding courses overlap from top to bottom so water will flow down over the surface without getting behind it.

Cricket. A peaked structure behind a chimney to prevent buildup of snow and ice that could cause leaks. The cricket is built like a small roof and is covered with roofing.

Cripple stud. A short stud above or below a door or window opening.

Crosscut. To saw a piece of lumber perpendicular to its length or its grain.

Cupping. A type of warping that causes the edges of a board to curl along its grain.

D

Dado joint. A joint formed when the end of one member fits into a groove cut partway through the face of another.

Dimension lumber. A piece of lumber that is at least 2 inches thick and at least 2 inches wide.

Drywall. A basic interior building material consisting of sheets of pressed gypsum faced with heavy paper on both sides. Also known as wallboard, gypsum board, plasterboard, and sheetrock.

E

Easement. A legal right for restricted use of someone's property. Easements often are granted to utility companies so they may service the utility lines running through a property.

Eaves. The lower edge of a roof that projects beyond the wall.

Edger. A concrete finishing tool for rounding and smoothing edges to strengthen them.

Edging. Strips of wood or veneer used to cover the edges of plywood or boards.

End grain. The ends of wood fibers that are exposed at the ends of boards, dimension lumber, or plywood.

Exposed aggregate surface. A concrete finish achieved by embedding aggregate into a concrete surface.

F

Fascia board. Horizontal trim attached to the outside ends of rafters or to the top of an exterior wall.

Finishing. The final smoothing stage in concrete work.

Flashing. Sheet metal or plastic sheets or strips used to form waterproof seals between surfaces or around openings on a roof or wall. Some flashings are preformed for specific purposes.

Float. A rectangular hand tool used to smooth and compress wet concrete. Also the first process of finishing a concrete surface.

Flush. On the same plane as, or level with, a surrounding surface.

Footing. A thick concrete support for walls and other heavy structures built on firm soil and extending below the frost line.

Framing. The skeletal or structural support of a building. Sometimes called framework.

Frost line. The maximum depth frost normally penetrates the soil during the winter. This depth varies with the climate from area to area.

G

Gable. The triangular area on an external wall defined by the sloping parts of a roof and a line between the roof's eaves.

Galvanized. Coated with a zinc outer covering to protect against oxidation. Nails and screws used in exterior applications often are galvanized to prevent them from rusting.

Grain. The direction of fibers in a piece of wood; also refers to the pattern of the fibers.

H–J

Hardwood. Lumber derived from deciduous trees such as oaks, maples, and walnuts.

Header. The framing component spanning a door or window opening in a wall and supporting the weight above it.

Hip. The angle formed by the intersection of two sloped surfaces of different pitch on the same side of a roof.

Inside corner. The point at which two walls form an internal angle, as in the corner of a room.

Jack studs. Studs at both sides of a door, window, or other opening that help support the header. Sometimes called trimmers.

Jamb. The top and side frames of a door or window opening.

Jointer. A tool used for making control joints, or grooves, in concrete surfaces to control cracking.

Joist. Horizontal framing member that supports a floor or ceiling.

K-L

Kerf. The slot left by a saw blade as it cuts through material.

King studs. Studs on both ends of a header that help support the header. They can run from the wall's sole plate to its top plate.

Lag screw. A screw, usually at least ¼ inch in diameter with a hexagonal head, that can be screwed in with a wrench rather than a screwdriver.

Lap joint. The joint formed when one member overlaps another.

Ledger. A horizontal support (usually lumber) that holds up the ends or edges of other members.

Level. The condition that exists when a surface is at true horizontal. Also a tool used to determine level.

Linear foot. A term used to refer to the length of a board or a piece of molding, in contrast to board foot.

Load-bearing wall. A wall that supports a wall or roof section on the floor above. Do not cut or remove a stud in a load-bearing wall without proper alternative support. See also *Partition wall.*

M-O

Miter joint. The joint formed when two members that have been cut at the same angle meet.

Molding. A strip of wood, usually small-dimensioned, used to cover exposed edges or as decoration.

Mortise. A shallow cutout in a piece of wood usually used to recess hardware such as door hinges and latches.

Nominal dimension. The identifying, reference size of lumber, such as 2×4. See also *Actual dimension.*

On center (OC). A measurement from the center of one regularly spaced framing member or hole to the center of the next.

One-by (two-by). Refers to nominal 1- or 2-inch-thick lumber of any width, length, or type of wood. Actual thicknesses are ¾ inch and 1½ inch, respectively.

Outside corner. The point at which two walls form an external angle; the corner you can usually walk around.

P-R

Partition wall. Unlike a load-bearing wall, a partition does not support a structure above it and can therefore be removed.

Pilot hole. A hole bored before driving a screw or nail to ensure against splitting the board. A pilot hole is slightly narrower than the fastener being driven through it.

Plumb. The condition that exists when a surface is at true vertical.

Pressure-treated wood. Lumber and sheet goods impregnated with one of several solutions to make the wood more impervious to moisture and rot.

Primer. A first coating formulated to seal raw surfaces and hold succeeding finish coats.

Rafters. Parallel framing members that support a roof.

Ready-mix. Concrete that is mixed in a truck as it is being delivered.

Rebar. Steel rod used to reinforce concrete and masonry. Also known as reinforcing rod and rerod.

Retaining wall. A wall constructed to hold soil in place.

Ridgeboard. Topmost beam at a roof's peak.

Rip. To saw lumber or sheet goods parallel to the grain.

Rise. The vertical distance from one point to another above it; a measurement you need to plan a stairway or ramp.

Riser. The upright piece between two stairsteps. See also *Tread.*

Rough-in. The early stages of a plumbing project during which supply and drain-waste-vent lines are run to their destinations.

Rough opening. The opening in the framing made to accommodate a door or window.

S

Sash. The part of a window that can be opened, consisting of a frame and glass.

Setback. The minimum distance permitted between a building and property lines (dictated by local zoning ordinances).

Setting nails. Driving the heads of nails slightly below the surface of the wood.

Shake. A shingle that has been split, rather than cut, from wood.

Sheathing. The first covering on a roof or exterior wall, usually fastened directly to the rafters or studs.

Shim. A thin piece of wood or other material used to fill a gap between two adjoining components or to help establish level or plumb.

Siding. Planks, boards, shingles, or sheet goods used as an external covering of the walls of a building.

Sill. The lowest horizontal piece of a window, door, or wall framework.

Soffit. Surfacing attached to the underside of eaves.

Softwood. Lumber derived from coniferous trees such as pines, firs, cedars, or redwoods.

Sole plate. The bottommost horizontal part of a stud-framed partition. When a plate rests on a foundation, it's called a sill plate.

Span. The distance between supports.

Square. The condition that exists when two surfaces are at 90 degrees to each other. Also a tool used to determine square.

Story pole. A board marked to show the courses of siding.

Stringer. The main structural member of a stairway.

Stucco. A mortar-based siding material applied with a trowel.

Studs. Vertical 2×4 or 2×6 framing members spaced at regular intervals within a wall.

Subfloor. Usually plywood or another sheet material covering the floor joists.

T-Z

Template. A pattern to follow when recreating a precise shape.

Timber. A structural or framing member that is 5 inches or larger in the smallest dimension.

Toenail. To drive a nail at an angle to hold together two pieces of material, usually studs in a wall.

Top plate. The topmost horizontal element of a stud-framed wall.

Tread. The level part of a staircase.

Truss. An engineered, prebuilt assembly of rafters and other framing members to support a roof.

Underlayment. A cementlike product that is used to level floors prior to laying surface material. Sometimes used to refer to a subfloor material or material laid on the subfloor. See also *Subfloor.*

Utility knife. A sharp knife with a retractable, replaceable blade.

Valley. An intersection of roof slopes.

Warp. Any of several lumber defects caused by uneven shrinkage of wood cells.

Zoning. Ordinances regulating the way in which property may be used. See also *Building code.*

index

live with *style*

Look for budget-friendly home improvements, smart decorating ideas, and space-saving solutions in these new Better Homes and Gardens® books.

Better Homes and Gardens®

An Imprint of ⊛ WILEY
Now you know.

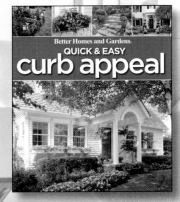

Better Homes and Gardens.
QUICK & EASY
curb appeal

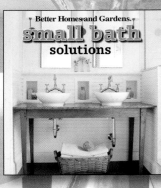

Better Homes and Gardens.
small bath
solutions

Better Homes and Gardens.
small kitchen
solutions

Better Homes and Gardens®
real-life decorating
Your Look, Your Budget

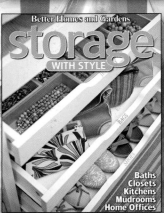

Better Homes and Gardens
storage WITH STYLE

Baths
Closets
Kitchens
Mudrooms
Home Offices

Better Homes and Gardens.
501 DECORATING **IDEAS** UNDER **$100**